The Golden Apples of the Sun

The Golde

Twentieth Centu

Edited by Chris Wallace-Crabbe

Apples of the Sun

Australian Poetry

MELBOURNE UNIVERSITY PRESS

1980

First published 1980
Typeset by The Dova Type Shop, Melbourne
Printed in Australia by
Wilke and Company Limited, Clayton, Victoria for
Melbourne University Press, Carlton, Victoria 3053
U.S.A. and Canada: International Scholarly Book Services, Inc.,
Box 555, Forest Grove, Oregon 97116
Great Britain, Europe, the Middle East, Africa and the Caribbean:
International Book Distributors Ltd (Prentice-Hall International)
66 Wood Lane End, Hemel Hempstead, Hertfordshire HP2 4RG,
England

National Library of Australia Cataloguing in Publication data
The golden apples of the sun.
    Index
    ISBN 0 522 84192 9

    1. Australian poetry. I. Wallace-Crabbe, Christopher,
    1934-, ed.
A821'.008

Contents

CONTENTS

CONTENTS

CONTENTS

CONTENTS

Introduction

While it has given me considerable delight to embark on a choice of the best, the most challenging and the most spirited Australian poems of this century, the sifting process has obviously been a difficult one and it has brought a number of general observations to mind. Accordingly, I want to offer a few of my reflections and conclusions before proceeding to the goods themselves.

H. M. Green, introducing his very distinguished and persuasive collection, *Modern Australian Poetry*, in 1946, pointed out that he was sampling a period which overlapped 'one of those rather indefinite boundaries that separate natural periods; the period of romantic nationalism and the period of modernity and disillusion, which faded into one another soon after the end of the first world war'. We can still say that western poetry finds its place within that mix, despite further pulses of secular modernism, those oblique, fashionable shock-waves of influence which have continued to make their impact felt in Australia.

The great landmark which stamps the beginning of twentieth century Australian poetry is Brennan's 'The Wanderer', itself in turn only designed as one segment of a larger composition, *Poems, 1913*. A profound inwardness begins with such lines as

> For this is the hard doom that is laid on all of you,
> to be that whereof you dream, dreaming against your will.

But modernism was treading hard on the heels of romanticism: this poem was begun in 1902 and already, in 1900, Freud had published *The Interpretation of Dreams*. The doom that was laid on all of us was a deeply reflexive one, indeed.

Inwardness is a quality which some commentators have felt to be lacking in most Australian verse, but there is plainly a line

1

of subtle, passionate introspection which runs from Brennan to Judith Wright, where it is felt as much in her *paysages moralisés* as in her lyrics of love and generation, to Francis Webb and to the Gwen Harwood who writes,

> I speak of those years when I lived
> walled alive in myself, left with nothing
> but the inward search for joy, for a word
> that would ruffle the plumage of mind to reach
> its tenderest down;

Webb's large contribution to this poetic strain might accurately be described as expressionist rather than reflective, but it was none the less the product of painful self-scrutiny. He has a central role in our modern tradition, linking back into the Sydney Lindsayites of the forties and forward to the generation of '68, many of whom took his work as their growing point.

Some of these new poets are hunting out the relation between surrealism and the logically necessary break-up of the unitary ego. Ern Malley, garage mechanic and fictitious genius of 1944, a modernist Ossian, was the first cruel punisher of this development: as a result of this notorious hoax, and despite some effects on the style of Banning, Harris and Webb, we had to wait for the surrealist steam-train to come clanking round a second time; it found the Tranter–Forbes generation waiting at the station with their discontents and their critique of all the assumptions of public rhetoric or of 'the discursive mode', to rehearse Hope's influential phrase. Instead of discourse we have Tranter cocking his snook at pieties, 'when we read *Das Kapital* between the jokes'.

But poetry with overt concerns is never wholly dead: far from it. The great public sentiments continue to call for expression and the throat of eloquence has not altogether been wrung. Thus we find the continuation of such a different strain of poetry as that represented by Manifold's 'The Tomb of Lt. John Learmonth, A.I.F.', Hope's 'In Memoriam: Gertrud Kolmar, 1943' and Dawe's 'Homecoming'. All these show how far war and arbitrary death remain significant keys to unlock the gates of poetry.

New, or neglected, themes can be seen to arise, too. Mary Gilmore saw early the significance of that compound ghost, the displaced Aboriginal culture, but for most of the century our poets have ignored what has remained for overseas observers the one truly distinctive feature of Australia. A mixture of anglophilia, cultural snobbery and fear has drawn a veil over the very existence of the Aborigines; we have contrived not to think about the complicated cultural patterns which they developed over millennia. The time has come now when Kath Walker has made her mark on 'our' poetry, when the sustained interest shown by Wright and Robinson in the lost ways is fully recognized, when the Jindyworobaks are no longer the butts of scorn, and when Les Murray can deliberately structure a long poem on the language patterns of an Aboriginal song cycle.

Much more familiar, and endlessly debated, has been the Australia–Europe tug-of-war. At one end of the rope it has given us the kind of excessive concentration on landscapes that typifies any suburban art show; at the other it gives us neo-classicism, the travellers' foreign cities and 'two gross of broken statues'. In between, it generates many flavours of comedy, sometimes reaching the pitch of bittersweet irony that fills Peter Porter's 'In the New World Happiness is Allowed'. But Malraux's imaginary museum of the modern mind also includes Asia, a continent which Australian poets have found remarkably hard to cope with, yearning as they have for Bloomsbury or Provence or Lower East Side. Harold Stewart and J. R. Rowland are among the very few whose imaginative, and real, residence in Asia has been deeply enough rooted to colour their work substantially, though Bruce Dawe has commented sardonically on our blindnesses in this area.

He, too, must be acclaimed for the restoration of suburbia, being the first poet since Slessor—even perhaps the very first—to look steadily on those stretched hundreds of square miles without contempt or patronage. And, despite the long-increasing habitation of the muses on university and college campuses, many poets have learned something from Dawe's gentle, humorous respect for common life. Even the new prankster-surrealism can dip its lid to that.

In the last resort, the central comedy of the Australian writers' world is surely the one which has been captured in the web of R. A. Simpson's atypical sestina, 'All Friends Together', the gaudy carousel of which whirls the same handful of names round again and again. Like any literature, ours must keep opening the doors on to a wider range of ideas and life-paths, for sheer health's sake.

The conflicts, the style-shifts, the warring schools which have sprung up among younger poets in the past dozen years are indicators of the substantial doubts many have about the very nature of poetry: of art at all, I should have said. On one side there are those who would still agree with Brennan that 'what is really taking place is an attempt to harmonize the world and the complete man' and on the other those who do not mind Gombrich's

claim that 'art has . . . become a social game played among art-
ists', so that all is jape and knowingness. Fortunately poems can
seize poets by the hair and carry them off—for all their pro-
grammes and poetics. All we can say, I believe, is that poetry
finds its being somewhere within the triangle whose three apices
are expression, knowledge and joy. And the greatest of these is
joy.

Finally I should declare certain principles which underlay my
selection of poems for this book. Above all, I chose poems first
and poets, alas, second. I wanted to use the poetry which interes-
ted me most deeply rather than seeking to represent careers or
bodies of work. Having completed the job, I remain satisfied
with this rule, but am aware that a few injustices have been done:
I can think of two or three impressive poets no single poem from
whom caught my eye or my ear sufficiently.

I have tried to keep long poems intact: snippets are not meals.
Further, I would have been happy to use more than I did. But
space is finite in this situation, so that some large works, by Webb
and FitzGerald, for instance, missed out and Buckley's 'Golden
Builders' is only here in part: enough, I hope, to give the true
taste of this urban anatomy.

Again, I decided to use no translations, such works lying some-
where between the imaginations of two people. This caused me
some regrets, in having to pass over Jack Hibberd's Baudelaire,
Philip Martin's Lars Gustafson and the translations of Mandel-
stam which have recently been coming from various hands in
Canberra. This rule has been bent in only one case: that of J. M.
Couper, whose Ocker surfie version of Horace moves so freely
away from the original model.

Finally, I hope that readers find the stimulation and variety
which I have had from these poems, produced over an eighty-
year span and all in my judgement having something to offer,
whether they be silver apples or golden apples or just plain black-
berries. In the end, poetry is not one thing; it is many things
with one generic label.

CHRIS WALLACE-CRABBE
Eltham, 1980

The silver apples of the moon,
The golden apples of the sun.

YEATS

An Aboriginal Simile

There was no stir among the trees,
No pulse in the earth,
No movement in the void;
The grass was a dry white fire.
Then in the distance rose a cloud,
And a swift rain came:
Like a woman running,
The wind in her hair.

Nationality

I have grown past hate and bitterness,
I see the world as one;
But though I can no longer hate,
My son is still my son.

All men at God's round table sit,
And all men must be fed;
But this loaf in my hand,
This loaf is my son's bread.

CHRISTOPHER BRENNAN

The Wanderer
1902—

Quoniam cor secretum concupivi
  factus sum vagus inter stellas huius revelationis:
Atque annus peregrinationis meae
  quasi annus ventorum invisibilium.

When window-lamps had dwindled, then I rose
and left the town behind me; and on my way
passing a certain door I stopt, remembering
how once I stood on its threshold, and my life
was offer'd to me, a road how different
from that of the years since gone! and I had but
to rejoin an olden path, once dear, since left.
All night I have walk'd and my heart was deep awake,
remembering ways I dream'd and that I chose,
remembering lucidly, and was not sad,
being brimm'd with all the liquid and clear dark
of the night that was not stirr'd with any tide;
for leaves were silent and the road gleam'd pale,
following the ridge, and I was alone with night.
But now I am come among the rougher hills
and grow aware of the sea that somewhere near
is restless; and the flood of night is thinn'd
and stars are whitening. O, what horrible dawn
will bare me the way and crude lumps of the hills
and the homeless concave of the day, and bare
the ever-restless, ever-complaining sea?

CHRISTOPHER BRENNAN

Each day I see the long ships coming into port
and the people crowding to their rail, glad of the shore:
because to have been alone with the sea and not to have
    known
of anything happening in any crowded way,
and to have heard no other voice than the crooning sea's
has charmed away the old rancours, and the great winds
have search'd and swept their hearts of the old irksome
    thoughts:
so, to their freshen'd gaze, each land smiles a good home.
Why envy I, seeing them made gay to greet the shore?
Surely I do not foolishly desire to go
hither and thither upon the earth and grow weary
with seeing many lands and peoples and the sea:
but if I might, some day, landing I reck not where
have heart to find a welcome and perchance a rest,
I would spread the sail to any wandering wind of the air
this night, when waves are hard and rain blots out the land.

I am driven everywhere from a clinging home,
O autumn eves! and I ween'd that you would yet
have made, when your smouldering dwindled to odorous
    fume,
close room for my heart, where I might crouch and dream
of days and ways I had trod, and look with regret
on the darkening homes of men and the window-gleam,
and forget the morrows that threat and the unknown way.
But a bitter wind came out of the yellow-pale west
and my heart is shaken and fill'd with its triumphing cry:
You shall find neither home nor rest: for ever you roam
with stars as they drift and wilful fates of the sky!

O tame heart, and why are you weary and cannot rest?
here is the hearth with its glow and the roof that forbids the
    rain,
a swept and a garnish'd quiet, a peace: and were you not fain
to be gather'd in dusk and comfort and barter away the rest?

[And is your dream . . .

CHRISTOPHER BRENNAN

And is your dream now of riding away from a stricken field
on a lost and baleful eve, when the world went out in rain,
one of some few that rode evermore by the bridle-rein
of a great beloved chief, with high heart never to yield?

Was that you? and you ween you are back in your life of old
when you dealt as your pride allow'd and reck'd not of other
    rein?
Nay, tame heart, be not idle: it is but the ancient rain
that minds you of manhood foregone and the perilous joy of
    the bold.

Once I could sit by the fire hourlong when the dripping eaves
sang cheer to the shelter'd, and listen, and know that the
    woods drank full,
and think of the morn that was coming and how the freshen'd
    leaves
would glint in the sun and the dusk beneath would be bright
    and cool.

Now, when I hear, I am cold within: for my mind drifts wide
where the blessing is shed for naught on the salt waste of the
    sea,
on the valleys that hold no rest and the hills that may not
    abide:
and the fire loses its warmth and my home is far from me.

How old is my heart, how old, how old is my heart,
and did I ever go forth with song when the morn was new?
I seem to have trod on many ways: I seem to have left
I know not how many homes; and to leave each
was still to leave a portion of mine own heart,
of my old heart whose life I had spent to make that home
and all I had was regret, and a memory.
So I sit and muse in this wayside harbour and wait
till I hear the gathering cry of the ancient winds and again
I must up and out and leave the embers of the hearth
to crumble silently into white ash and dust,

and see the road stretch bare and pale before me: again
my garment and my home shall be the enveloping winds
and my heart be fill'd wholly with their old pitiless cry.

I sorrow for youth—ah, not for its wildness (would that were
    dead!)
but for those soft nests of time that enticed the maiden bloom
of delight and tenderness to break in delicate air
—O her eyes in the rosy face that bent over our first babe!
but all that was, and is gone, and shall be all forgotten;
it fades and wanes even now: and who is there cares but I?
and I grieve for my heart that is old and cannot cease from
    regret.
Ay, might our harms be haven'd in some deathless heart:
but where have I felt its over-brooding luminous tent
save in those eyes of delight (and ah! that they must change)
and of yore in her eyes to whom we ran with our childish joy?
O brother! if such there were and each of us might lead each
to lean above the little pools where all our heart
lies spilt and clear and shining along the dusky way,
and dream of one that could save it all and salve our ache!

You, at whose table I have sat, some distant eve
beside the road, and eaten and you pitied me
to be driven an aimless way before the pitiless winds,
how much ye have given and knew not, pitying foolishly!
For not alone the bread I broke, but I tasted too
all your unwitting lives and knew the narrow soul
that bodies it in the landmarks of your fields,
and broods dumbly within your little seasons' round,
where, after sowing, comes the short-lived summer's mirth,
and, after harvesting, the winter's lingering dream,
half memory and regret, half hope, crouching beside
the hearth that is your only centre of life and dream.
And knowing the world how limitless and the way how long,
and the home of man how feeble and builded on the winds,
I have lived your life, that eve, as you might never live
knowing, and pity you, if you should come to know.

CHRISTOPHER BRENNAN

I cry to you as I pass your windows in the dusk;

Ye have built you unmysterious homes and ways in the wood
where of old ye went with sudden eyes to the right and left;
and your going was now made safe and your staying
    comforted,
for the forest edge itself, holding old savagery
in unsearch'd glooms, was your houses' friendly barrier.
And now that the year goes winterward, ye thought to hide
behind your gleaming panes, and where the hearth sings
    merrily
make cheer with meat and wine, and sleep in the long night,
and the uncared wastes might be a crying unhappiness.
But I, who have come from the outer night, I say to you
the winds are up and terribly will they shake the dry wood:
the woods shall awake, hearing them, shall awake to be toss'd
    and riven,
and make a cry and a parting in your sleep all night
as the wither'd leaves go whirling all night along all ways.
And when ye come forth at dawn, uncomforted by sleep,
ye shall stand at amaze, beholding all the ways overhidden
with worthless drift of the dead and all your broken world:
and ye shall not know whence the winds have come, nor shall
    ye know
whither the yesterdays have fled, or if they were.

Come out, come out, ye souls that serve, why will ye die?
or will ye sit and stifle in your prison-homes
dreaming of some master that holds the winds in leash
and the waves of darkness yonder in the gaunt hollow of
    night?
nay, there is none that rules: all is a strife of the winds
and the night shall billow in storm full oft ere all be done.
For this is the hard doom that is laid on all of you,
to be that whereof ye dream, dreaming against your will.
But first ye must travel the many ways, and your close-wrapt
    souls
must be blown thro' with the rain that comes from the
    homeless dark:

for until ye have had care of the wastes there shall be no truce
for them nor you, nor home, but ever the ancient feud;
and the soul of man must house the cry of the darkling waves
as he follows the ridge above the waters shuddering towards
      night,
and the rains and the winds that roam anhunger'd for some
      heart's warmth.
Go: tho' ye find it bitter, yet must ye be bare
to the wind and the sea and the night and the wail of birds in
      the sky;
go: tho' the going be hard and the goal blinded with rain
yet the staying is a death that is never soften'd with sleep.

Dawns of the world, how I have known you all,
so many, and so varied, and the same!
dawns o'er the timid plains, or in the folds .
of the arm'd hills, or by the unsleeping shore;
a chill touch on the chill flesh of the dark
that, shuddering, shrinks from its couch, and leaves
a homeless light, staring, disconsolate,
on the drear world it knows too well, the world
it fled and finds again, its wistful hope
unmet by any miracle of night,
that mocks it rather, with its shreds that hang
about the woods and huddled bulks of gloom
that crouch, malicious, in the broken combes,
witness to foulnesses else unreveal'd
that visit earth and violate her dreams
in the lone hours when only evil wakes.

What is there with you and me, that I may not forget
but your white shapes come crowding noiselessly in my nights,
making my sleep a flight from a thousand beckoning hands?
Was it not enough that your cry dwelt in my waking ears
that now, seeking oblivion, I must yet be haunted
by each black maw of hunger that yawns despairingly
a moment ere its whitening frenzy bury it?

                    [O waves of all the seas, . . .

CHRISTOPHER BRENNAN

O waves of all the seas, would I could give you peace
and find my peace again: for all my peace is fled
and broken and blown along your white delirious crests!

O desolate eves along the way, how oft,
despite your bitterness, was I warm at heart!
not with the glow of remember'd hearths, but warm
with the solitary unquenchable fire that burns
a flameless heat deep in his heart who has come
where the formless winds plunge and exult for aye
among the naked spaces of the world,
far past the circle of the ruddy hearths
and all their memories. Desperate eves;
when the wind-bitten hills turn'd violet
along their rims, and the earth huddled her heat
within her niggard bosom, and the dead stones
lay battle-strewn before the iron wind
that, blowing from the chill west, made all its way
a loneliness to yield its triumph room;
yet in that wind a clamour of trumpets rang,
old trumpets, resolute, stark, undauntable,
singing to battle against the eternal foe,
the wronger of this world, and all his powers
in some last fight, foredoom'd disastrous,
upon the final ridges of the world:
a war-won note, stern fire in the stricken eve,
and fire thro' all my ancient heart, that sprang
towards that last hope of a glory won in defeat,
whence, knowing not sure if such high grace befall
at the end, yet I draw courage to front the way.

The land I came thro' last was dumb with night,
a limbo of defeated glory, a ghost:
for wreck of constellations flicker'd perishing
scarce sustain'd in the mortuary air,
and on the ground and out of livid pools
wreck of old swords and crowns glimmer'd at whiles;
I seem'd at home in some old dream of kingship:

now it is clear grey day and the road is plain,
I am the wanderer of many years
who cannot tell if ever he was king
or if ever kingdoms were: I know I am
the wanderer of the ways of all the worlds,
to whom the sunshine and the rain are one
and one to stay or hasten, because he knows
no ending of the way, no home, no goal,
and phantom night and the grey day alike
withhold the heart where all my dreams and days
might faint in soft fire and delicious death:
and saying this to myself as a simple thing
I feel a peace fall in the heart of the winds
and a clear dusk settle, somewhere, far in me.

'The point of noon is past'

The point of noon is past, outside: light is asleep;
brooding upon its perfect hour: the woods are deep
and solemn, fill'd with unseen presences of light
that glint, allure, and hide them; ever yet more bright
(it seems) the turn of a path will show them: nay, but rest;
seek not, and think not; dream, and know not; this is best:
the hour is full; be lost: whispering, the woods are bent,
This is the only revelation; be content.

The Orange Tree

The young girl stood beside me. I
   Saw not what her young eyes could see:
—A light, she said, not of the sky
   Lives somewhere in the Orange Tree.

—Is it, I said, of east or west?
   The heartbeat of a luminous boy
Who with his faltering flute confessed
   Only the edges of his joy?

Was he, I said, borne to the blue
   In a mad escapade of Spring
Ere he could make a fond adieu
   To his love in the blossoming?

—Listen! the young girl said. There calls
   No voice, no music beats on me;
But it is almost sound: it falls
   This evening on the Orange Tree.

—Does he, I said, so fear the Spring
   Ere the white sap too far can climb?
See in the full gold evening
   All happenings of the olden time?

Is he so goaded by the green?
   Does the compulsion of the dew
Make him unknowable but keen
   Asking with beauty of the blue?

—Listen! the young girl said. For all
   Your hapless talk you fail to see
There is a light, a step, a call,
   This evening on the Orange Tree.

—Is it, I said, a waste of love
    Imperishably old in pain,
Moving as an affrighted dove
    Under the sunlight or the rain?

Is it a fluttering heart that gave
    Too willingly and was reviled?
Is it the stammering at a grave,
    The last word of a little child?

—Silence! the young girl said. Oh, why,
    Why will you talk to weary me?
Plague me no longer now, for I
    Am listening like the Orange Tree.

Song be Delicate

Let your song be delicate.
    The skies declare
No war—the eyes of lovers
    Wake everywhere.

Let your voice be delicate.
    How faint a thing
Is Love, little Love crying
    Under the Spring.

Let your song be delicate.
    The flowers can hear:
Too well they know the tremble,
    Of the hollow year.

Let your voice be delicate.
    The bees are home:
All their day's love is sunken
    Safe in the comb.

[Let your song be . . .

Let your song be delicate.
    Sing no loud hymn:
Death is abroad . . . oh, the black season!
    The deep—the dim!

Native Companions Dancing

On the blue plains in wintry days
    These stately birds move in the dance.
Keen eyes have they, and quaint old ways
On the blue plains in wintry days.
The Wind, their unseen Piper, plays,
    They strut, salute, retreat, advance;
On the blue plains, in wintry days,
    These stately birds move in the dance.

May

Shyly the silver-hatted mushrooms make
    Soft entrance through,
And undelivered lovers, half awake,
    Hear noises in the dew.

Yellow in all the earth and in the skies,
    The world would seem
Faint as a widow mourning with soft eyes
    And falling into dream.

Up the long hill I see the slow plough leave
    Furrows of brown;
Dim is the day and beautiful: I grieve
    To see the sun go down.

JOHN SHAW NEILSON

But there are suns a many for mine eyes
   Day after day:
Delightsome in grave greenery they rise,
   Red oranges in May.

HUGH McCRAE

Fragment

As if stone Caesar shook
His staff across the wet
Black passages, and took
With marble eyes a yet
Unconquered gaze of Rome;
Marked how the cypress boughs
Stood thick about his home
As when he bent his brows
Three centuries before
Across some Gordian knot
His civic business wore—
Hic jacet the whole lot.

What hammer fell? And whose
The crushed white paper skull
Mixed in the side-bank ooze
Of mighty Tiber . . . Dull
The mind and hand that first
Wrought sparth and sinker-blade,
Knobbed clubs and spikes to burst
The fairy spirit from the shade

                                   [He entered in, . . .

HUGH McCRAE

He entered in, when through a mesh
Of aching tissues, blood to blood,
And flesh on softly folding flesh,
Man with his woman made a flood
Of kings and weavers, so the world
Might fling about in sunny ways,
Some to the hunt, and some, up-curled,
Stung silent in the martyr's blaze.

VANCE PALMER

The Farmer remembers the Somme

Will they never fade or pass!
The mud, and the misty figures endlessly coming
In file through the foul morass,
And the grey flood-water lipping the reeds and grass,
And the steel wings drumming.

The hills are bright in the sun:
There's nothing changed or marred in the well-known places;
When work for the day is done
There's talk, and quiet laughter, and gleams of fun
On the old folks' faces.

I have returned to these:
The farm, and the kindly Bush, and the young calves lowing;
But all that my mind sees
Is a quaking bog in a mist—stark, snapped trees,
And the dark Somme flowing.

The Night-ride

Gas flaring on the yellow platform; voices running up and
   down;
Milk-tins in cold dented silver; half-awake I stare,
Pull up the blind, blink out—all sounds are drugged;
The slow blowing of passengers asleep;
Engines yawning; water in heavy drips;
Black, sinister travellers, lumbering up the station,
One moment in the window, hooked over bags;
Hurrying, unknown faces—boxes with strange labels—
All groping clumsily to mysterious ends,
Out of the gaslight, dragged by private Fates.
Their echoes die. The dark train shakes and plunges;
Bells cry out; the night-ride starts again.
Soon I shall look out into nothing but blackness,
Pale, windy fields. The old roar and knock of the rails
Melts in dull fury. Pull down the blind. Sleep. Sleep.
Nothing but grey, rushing rivers of bush outside.
Gaslight and milk-cans. Of Rapptown I recall nothing else.

South Country

After the whey-faced anonymity
Of river-gums and scribbly-gums and bush,
After the rubbing and the hit of brush,
You come to the South Country

As if the argument of trees were done,
The doubts and quarrelling, the plots and pains,
All ended by these clear and gliding planes
Like an abrupt solution.

            [And over the flat earth . . .

And over the flat earth of empty farms
The monstrous continent of air floats back
Coloured with rotting sunlight and the black,
Bruised flesh of thunderstorms:

Air arched, enormous, pounding the bony ridge,
Ditches and hutches, with a drench of light,
So huge, from such infinities of height,
You walk on the sky's beach

While even the dwindled hills are small and bare,
As if, rebellious, buried, pitiful,
Something below pushed up a knob of skull,
Feeling its way to air.

Captain Dobbin

Captain Dobbin, having retired from the South Seas
In the dumb tides of 1900, with a handful of shells,
A few poisoned arrows, a cask of pearls,
And five thousand pounds in the colonial funds,
Now sails the street in a brick villa, 'Laburnum Villa',
In whose blank windows the harbour hangs
Like a fog against the glass,
Golden and smoky, or stoned with a white glitter,
And boats go by, suspended in the pane,
Blue Funnel, Red Funnel, Messageries Maritimes,
Lugged down the port like sea-beasts taken alive
That scrape their bellies on sharp sands,
Of which particulars Captain Dobbin keeps
A ledger sticky with ink,
Entries of time and weather, state of the moon,
Nature of cargo and captain's name,
For some mysterious and awful purpose
Never divulged.
For at night, when the stars mock themselves with lanterns,
So late the chimes blow loud and faint

KENNETH SLESSOR

Like a hand shutting and unshutting over the bells,
Captain Dobbin, having observed from bed
The lights, like a great fiery snake, of the *Comorin*
Going to sea, will note the hour
For subsequent recording in his gazette.

But the sea is really closer to him than this,
Closer to him than a dead, lovely woman,
For he keeps bits of it, like old letters,
Salt tied up in bundles
Or pressed flat,
What you might call a lock of the sea's hair,

So Captain Dobbin keeps his dwarfed memento,
His urn-burial, a chest of mummied waves,
Gales fixed in print, and the sweet dangerous countries
Of shark and casuarina-tree,
Stolen and put in coloured maps,
Like a flask of seawater, or a bottled ship,
A schooner caught in a glass bottle;
But Captain Dobbin keeps them in books,
Crags of varnished leather
Pimply with gilt, by learned mariners
And masters of hydrostatics, or the childish tales
Of simple heroes, taken by Turks or dropsy.
So nightly he sails from shelf to shelf
Or to the quadrants, dangling with rusty screws,
Or the hanging-gardens of old charts,
So old they bear the authentic protractor-lines,
Traced in faint ink, as fine as Chinese hairs.

Over the flat and painted atlas-leaves
His reading-glass would tremble,
Over the fathoms, pricked in tiny rows,
Water shelving to the coast.
Quietly the bone-rimmed lens would float
Till, through the glass, he felt the barbèd rush
Of bubbles foaming, spied the albicores,
The blue-finned admirals, heard the wind-swallowed cries

[Of planters running . . .

Of planters running on the beach
Who filched their swags of yams and ambergris,
Birds' nests and sandalwood, from pastures numbed
By the sun's yellow, too meek for honest theft;
But he, less delicate robber, climbed the walls,
Broke into dozing houses
Crammed with black bottles, marish wine
Crusty and salt-corroded, fading prints,
Sparkle-daubed almanacs and playing cards,
With rusty cannon, left by the French outside,
Half-buried in sand,
Even to the castle of Queen Pomaree
In the Yankee's footsteps, and found her throne-room piled
With golden candelabras, mildewed swords,
Guitars and fowling-pieces, tossed in heaps
With greasy cakes and flung-down calabashes.

Then Captain Dobbin's eye,
That eye of wild and wispy scudding blue,
Voluptuously prying, would light up
Like mica scratched by gully-suns,
And he would be fearful to look upon
And shattering in his conversation;
Nor would he tolerate the harmless chanty,
No '*Shenandoah*', or the dainty mew
That landsmen offer in a silver dish
To Neptune, sung to pianos in candlelight.
Of these he spoke in scorn,
For there was but one way of singing '*Stormalong*',
He said, and that was not really singing,
But howling, rather—shrieked in the wind's jaws
By furious men; not tinkled in drawing-rooms
By lap-dogs in clean shirts.
And, at these words,
The galleries of photographs, men with rich beards,
Pea-jackets and brass buttons, with folded arms,
Would scowl approval, for they were shipmates, too,
Companions of no cruise by reading-glass,
But fellows of storm and honey from the past—
'The Charlotte, Java, '93',
'Knuckle and Fred at Port au Prince',

'William in his New Rig',
Even that notorious scoundrel, Captain Baggs,
Who, as all knew, owed Dobbin Twenty Pounds
Lost at fair cribbage, but he never paid,
Or paid 'with the slack of the tops'l sheets'
As Captain Dobbin frequently expressed it.

There were their faces, grilled a trifle now,
Cigar-hued in various spots
By the brown breath of sodium-eating years,
On quarter-decks long burnt to the water's edge,
A resurrection of the dead by chemicals.
And the voyages they had made,
Their labours in a country of water,
Were they not marked by inadequate lines
On charts tied up like skins in a rack?
Or his own Odysseys, his lonely travels,
His trading days, an autobiography
Of angles and triangles and lozenges
Ruled tack by tack across the sheet,
That with a single scratch expressed the stars,
Merak and Alamak and Alpherat,
The wind, the moon, the sun, the clambering sea,

Sails bleached with light, salt in the eyes,
Bamboos and Tahiti oranges,
From some forgotten countless day,
One foundered day from a forgotten month,
A year sucked quietly from the blood,
Dead with the rest, remembered by no more
Than a scratch on a dry chart—
Or when the return grew too choking bitter-sweet
And laburnum-berries manifestly tossed
Beyond the window, not the fabulous leaves
Of Hotoo or canoe-tree or palmetto,
There were the wanderings of other keels,
Magellan, Bougainville and Cook,
Who found no greater a memorial
Than footprints over a lithograph.

[For Cook he worshipped, . . .

For Cook he worshipped, that captain with the sad
And fine white face, who never lost a man
Or flinched a peril; and of Bougainville
He spoke with graceful courtesy, as a rival
To whom the honours of the hunting-field
Must be accorded. Not so with the Spaniard,
Sebastian Juan del Cano, at whom he sneered
Openly, calling him a fool of fortune
Blown to a sailors' abbey by chance winds
And blindfold currents, who slept in a fine cabin,
Blundered through five degrees of latitude,
Was bullied by mutineers a hundred more,
And woke and found himself across the world.

Coldly in the window,
Like a fog rubbed up and down the glass
The harbour, bony with mist
And ropes of water, glittered; and the blind tide
That crawls it knows not where, nor for what gain,
Pushed its drowned shoulders against the wheel,
Against the wheel of the mill.
Flowers rocked far down
And white, dead bodies that were anchored there
In marshes of spent light.
Blue Funnel, Red Funnel,
The ships went over them, and bells in engine-rooms
Cried to their bowels of flaring oil,
And stokers groaned and sweated with burnt skins,
Clawed to their shovels.
But quietly in his room,
In his little cemetery of sweet essences
With fond memorial-stones and lines of grace,
Captain Dobbin went on reading about the sea.

Sleep

Do you give yourself to me utterly,
   Body and no-body, flesh and no-flesh,

Not as a fugitive, blindly or bitterly,
    But as a child might, with no other wish?
Yes, utterly.

Then I shall bear you down my estuary,
Carry you and ferry you to burial mysteriously,
Take you and receive you,
Consume you, engulf you,
In the huge cave, my belly, lave you
With huger waves continually.

And you shall cling and clamber there
And slumber there, in that dumb chamber,
Beat with my blood's beat, hear my heart move
Blindly in bones that ride above you,
Delve in my flesh, dissolved and bedded,
Through viewless valves embodied so—

Till daylight, the expulsion and awakening,
    The riving and the driving forth,
Life with remorseless forceps beckoning—
    Pangs and betrayal of harsh birth.

Five Bells

Time that is moved by little fidget wheels
Is not my Time, the flood that does not flow.
Between the double and the single bell
Of a ship's hour, between a round of bells
From the dark warship riding there below,
I have lived many lives, and this one life
Of Joe, long dead, who lives between five bells.

[Deep and dissolving . . .

Deep and dissolving verticals of light
Ferry the falls of moonshine down. Five bells
Coldly rung out in a machine's voice. Night and water
Pour to one rip of darkness, the Harbour floats
In air, the Cross hangs upside-down in water.

Why do I think of you, dead man, why thieve
These profitless lodgings from the flukes of thought
Anchored in Time? You have gone from earth,
Gone even from the meaning of a name;
Yet something's there, yet something forms its lips
And hits and cries against the ports of space,
Beating their sides to make its fury heard.

Are you shouting at me, dead man, squeezing your face
In agonies of speech on speechless panes?
Cry louder, beat the windows, bawl your name!

But I hear nothing, nothing . . . only bells,
Five bells, the bumpkin calculus of Time.
Your echoes die, your voice is dowsed by Life,
There's not a mouth can fly the pygmy strait—
Nothing except the memory of some bones
Long shoved away, and sucked away, in mud;
And unimportant things you might have done,
Or once I thought you did; but you forgot,
And all have now forgotten—looks and words
And slops of beer; your coat with buttons off,
Your gaunt chin and pricked eye, and raging tales
Of Irish kings and English perfidy,
And dirtier perfidy of publicans
Groaning to God from Darlinghurst.
                                        Five bells.

Then I saw the road, I heard the thunder
Tumble, and felt the talons of the rain
The night we came to Moorebank in slab-dark,
So dark you bore no body, had no face,
But a sheer voice that rattled out of air
(As now you'd cry if I could break the glass),
A voice that spoke beside me in the bush,

Loud for a breath or bitten off by wind,
Of Milton, melons, and the Rights of Man,
And blowing flutes, and how Tahitian girls
Are brown and angry-tongued, and Sydney girls
Are white and angry-tongued, or so you'd found.
But all I heard was words that didn't join
So Milton became melons, melons girls,
And fifty mouths, it seemed, were out that night,
And in each tree an Ear was bending down,
Or something had just run, gone behind grass,
When, blank and bone-white, like a maniac's thought,
The naphtha-flash of lightning slit the sky,
Knifing the dark with deathly photographs.
There's not so many with so poor a purse
Or fierce a need, must fare by night like that,
Five miles in darkness on a country track,
But when you do, that's what you think.

Five bells.

In Melbourne, your appetite had gone,
Your angers too; they had been leeched away
By the soft archery of summer rains
And the sponge-paws of wetness, the slow damp
That stuck the leaves of living, snailed the mind,
And showed your bones, that had been sharp with rage,
The sodden ecstasies of rectitude.
I thought of what you'd written in faint ink,
Your journal with the sawn-off lock, that stayed behind
With other things you left, all without use,
All without meaning now, except a sign
That someone had been living who now was dead:
'At Labassa. Room 6 x 8
On top of the tower; because of this, very dark
And cold in winter. Everything has been stowed
Into this room—500 books all shapes
And colours, dealt across the floor
And over sills and on the laps of chairs;
Guns, photoes of many differant things
And differant curioes that I obtained . . .'

[In Sydney, by the . . .

In Sydney, by the spent aquarium-flare
Of penny gaslight on pink wallpaper,
We argued about blowing up the world,
But you were living backwards, so each night
You crept a moment closer to the breast,
And they were living, all of them, those frames
And shapes of flesh that had perplexed your youth,
And most your father, the old man gone blind,
With fingers always round a fiddle's neck,
That graveyard mason whose fair monuments
And tablets cut with dreams of piety
Rest on the bosoms of a thousand men
Staked bone by bone, in quiet astonishment
At cargoes they had never thought to bear,
These funeral-cakes of sweet and sculptured stone.

Where have you gone? The tide is over you,
The turn of midnight water's over you,
As Time is over you, and mystery,
And memory, the flood that does not flow.
You have no suburb, like those easier dead
In private berths of dissolution laid—
The tide goes over, the waves ride over you
And let their shadows down like shining hair,
But they are Water; and the sea-pinks bend
Like lilies in your teeth, but they are Weed;
And you are only part of an Idea.
I felt the wet push its black thumb-balls in,
The night you died, I felt your eardrums crack,
And the short agony, the longer dream,
The Nothing that was neither long nor short;
But I was bound, and could not go that way,
But I was blind, and could not feel your hand.
If I could find an answer, could only find
Your meaning, or could say why you were here
Who now are gone, what purpose gave you breath
Or seized it back, might I not hear your voice?

I looked out of my window in the dark
At waves with diamond quills and combs of light
That arched their mackerel-backs and smacked the sand

In the moon's drench, that straight enormous glaze,
And ships far off asleep, and Harbour-buoys
Tossing their fireballs wearily each to each,
And tried to hear your voice, but all I heard
Was a boat's whistle, and the scraping squeal
Of seabirds' voices far away, and bells,
Five bells. Five bells coldly ringing out.

Five bells.

Beach Burial

Softly and humbly to the Gulf of Arabs
The convoys of dead sailors come;
At night they sway and wander in the waters far under,
But morning rolls them in the foam.

Between the sob and clubbing of the gunfire
Someone, it seems, has time for this,
To pluck them from the shallows and bury them in burrows
And tread the sand upon their nakedness;

And each cross, the driven stake of tidewood,
Bears the last signature of men,
Written with such perplexity, with such bewildered pity,
The words choke as they begin—

'*Unknown seaman*'—the ghostly pencil
Wavers and fades, the purple drips,
The breath of the wet season has washed their inscriptions
As blue as drowned men's lips,

Dead seamen, gone in search of the same landfall,
Whether as enemies they fought,
Or fought with us, or neither; the sand joins them together,
Enlisted on the other front.

El Alamein.

ROBERT D. FITZGERALD

The Face of the Waters

Once again the scurry of feet—those myriads
crossing the black granite; and again
laughter cruelly in pursuit; and then
the twang like a harpstring or the spring of a trap,
and the swerve on the polished surface: the soft little pads
sidling and skidding and avoiding; but soon caught up
in the hand of laughter and put back . . .

There is no release from the rack
of darkness for the unformed shape,
the unexisting thought
stretched half-and-half
in the shadow of beginning and that denser black
under the imminence of huge pylons—
the deeper nought;
but neither is there anything to escape,
or to laugh,
or to twang that string which is not a string but silence
plucked at the heart of silence.

Nor can there be a floor to the bottomless;
except in so far as conjecture must arrive,
lungs cracking, at the depth of its dive;
where downward further is further distress
with no change in it; as if a mile and an inch
are equally squeezed into a pinch,
and retreating limits of cold mind
frozen, smoothed, defined.

Out of the tension of silence (the twanged string);
from the agony of not being (that terrible laughter
tortured by darkness); out of it all
once again the tentative migration; once again
a universe on the edge of being born:
feet running fearfully out of nothing
at the core of nothing:
colour, light, life, fearfully
becoming eyes and understanding: sound becoming ears . . .

ROBERT D. FITZGERALD

For eternity is not space reaching
on without end to it; not time without end to it,
nor infinity working round in a circle;
but a placeless dot enclosing nothing,
the pre-time pinpoint of impossible beginning,
enclosed by nothing, not even by emptiness—
impossible: so wholly at odds with possibilities
that, always emergent and wrestling and interlinking
they shatter it and return to it, are all of it and part of it.
It is your hand stretched out to touch your neighbour's,
and feet running through the dark, directionless like darkness.

Worlds that were spun adrift re-enter
that intolerable centre;
indeed the widest-looping comet
never departed from it;
it alone exists.
And though, opposing it, there persists
the enormous structure of forces, laws,
as background for other coming and going,
that's but a pattern, a phase, no pause,
of ever-being-erected, ever-growing
ideas unphysically alternative
to nothing, which is the quick. You may say hills live,
or life's the imperfect aspect of a flowing
that sorts itself as hills; much as thoughts wind
selectively through mind.

The egg-shell collapses
in the fist of the eternal instant;
all is what it was before.
Yet is that eternal instant
the pinpoint bursting into reality,
the possibilities and perhapses,
the feet scurrying on the floor.
It is the suspense also
with which the outward thrust
holds the inward surrender—
the stresses in the shell before it buckles under:
the struggle to magpie-morning and all life's clamour and lust;
the part breaking through the whole;
light and the clear day and so simple a goal.

ROBERT D. FITZGERALD

Fifth Day

In William Rufus's hall the galleries reached
half to the rafters like a roost for lords,
perching the fashion of England; back seats fetched
more than a nabob's bribe. The season affords
nothing so sought as these hard boards;
so rustling ladies, crush your muslin frocks . . .
There's Mrs Fitzherbert in the royal box.

Scarlet and ermine judges, wigs, gold laces,
canopies, woolsacks, drapings in red and green
for Peers' benches and Commons'—the culprit faces
a canvas not a court, a painted scene;
and from the obsolete frame there lean
figures trapped for tomorrow: history hooks
the observer into its foreground while he looks.

The proclamation for silence! Silence lies deep
under two hundred years. Almost you would say
the heralds are varnished over, standing asleep,
and the voice demanding silence has echoed away
far into silence. As if that day
were flat, still surface at last. But there survives
a hand in the midst, turning old thoughts, old lives.

Quill-marks migrate across a writing-block—
it is Joseph Gurney's hand. He heads his page:
'Fifth day: it wants a quarter of twelve o'clock:
the Chancellor presides'; so sets a stage
where words must jostle and engage
and die on utterance. But as they pass
paper shall catch their breaths like fog on glass.

'Warren Hastings Esquire, come forth in court
to save thee and thy bail' . . . Seven years shall run;
but a verdict will not end it—would a report
settle affairs in India, cool that sun
that policies well and ill begun
curve about since da Gama? Britain was built
round India and on Hastings—prove his guilt!

ROBERT D. FITZGERALD

'Charges of misdemeanours and high crimes'—
prove—if proved, share them! Long ago, far hence,
they are drowned under the influx of new times.
What's done goes on for ever as consequence;
but there's some blurring of evidence
by happenings more at elbow. Why try this man?
Hastings is no concern of Pakistan.

But it concerns all men that what they do
remains significant unbroken thread
of the fabric of our living. A man spoke so,
and acted so; and everything done or said
is superseded and overlaid
by change of time and pattern. Be that as it may,
there was need he lift his finger, say his say.

Attitude matters: bearing. Action in the end
goes down the stream as motion, merges as such
with the whole of life and time; but islands stand:
dignity and distinctness that attach
to the inmost being of us each.
It matters for man's private respect that still
face differs from face and will from will.

It is important how men looked and were.
Infirm, staggering a little, as Hastings was,
his voice was steady as his eyes. Kneeling at the bar
(ruler but late of millions) had steeled his poise;
he fronted inescapable loss
and thrown, stinking malice and disrepute,
calmly, a plain man in a plain suit.

Undersized, spare, licked dry by tropic heat;
one, with severe forehead and hard lips,
who had taken age's shilling and complete
grey uniform though not its grey eclipse—
with movements like commands, like whips:
here is the centre, whether for applause or loathing,
when evidence and acquittal alike mean nothing.

                    [But the eye strays . . .

But the eye strays from centre. The axle's part
is just to endure the play and spin of the spokes.
It is another figure rouses the heart,
a scholar loving his nation above his books,
who, pushed by a conscience that provokes
past reason or discretion, steps, half blind,
to darkness of anger from great light of his mind.

A compact, muscular man warms to the work
which will embitter him in another's feud,
his own mission and error. Edmund Burke
for right's clear sake is hounding his pursued,
inveterate, through this seven years' cloud
where subtle poison—Francis—steeps him whole;
he stands at the middle of the floor and twists his scroll.

'My lords, the gentlemen whom the Commons appoint
to manage this prosecution direct me thus
to inform your lordships'. . . . The cool phrases joint
one into other, and clause links on clause
wrought arguments whereby the cause
of justice and upright dealing may extend
from Westminster to India, and beyond.

Pitt sits near Fox and the managers, listens and learns.
Burke's heavy features liven with that magic
under them and their spectacles, which turns
knowledge to vision, and vision to strategic
marshalling of words and march of logic
through illustrations like landscapes and up steep
Quebec heights of statistics. Fox is asleep.

Francis is awake—behind the mask of his face,
inscrutable . . . as Junius. 'I have found,'
Hastings had said, 'in private as in his place,
he is void of truth and honour.' But cards go round;
brilliant, elegant as unsound,
he is one to hold them craftily, lead them well;
Hastings is now his victim, Burke his tool.

Something is eternal in the tugging of minds
which is not in mountains or monuments maturing
through day and darkness of centuries; something that binds
life into tensions and balances enduring
amid flowers withering and years flowering;
whereby in the instant of contest men outlive
upshots that melt in hot hands that achieve.

The fifth day wore to its close. On his feet still,
Burke was become tired body, who was cold brain
of impersonal Accusation. Suddenly ill,
he suddenly was himself, forcing through pain
words that seemed far off and in vain—
empty things scattered about by someone else,
a child dressed up in a bob-wig, playing with shells.

That moment swallows everything, like the gulf
two hundred years are hushed in: the fatigues
that buzzed like sickness in his brain: the trial itself
which was a swarming of motives and intrigues.
All the antagonisms, leagues,
plots and pamphlets are folded up, collapse;
but still the persons move, the drama shapes.

Here is displayed failure. Though there ensues
a recovery, a tomorrow that shall atone—
another hour, when Burke's voice shall cry: 'Choose!'
and he shall stand in England almost alone,
weighing a guillotine and a throne—
results mean little; they cancel and coalesce.
A gesture will outweigh them, a trick of dress.

The common work outweighs them—the anonymous gift
to the future, living, widening. What indeed
of that old struggle matters or would be left
but for an ordinary fellow's simple need,
who had a family to feed
and liked going to church looked up to, known
as a man with a tidy business of his own?

[Fox hurried to . . .

Fox hurried to Burke's aid. The court adjourned.
Gurney stoppered his inkhorn, wiped his pen . . .
Poor Mr Burke! But it was money earned
lightly and sweetened labour, for lesser men,
to go home early now and then.
Tuck today under an arm—though Hastings bent
that frown, there remained but shorthand. He bowed and went.

Beginnings

Not to have known the hard-bitten,
tight-lipped Caesar
clamped down on savage Britain;
or, moving closer,
not to have watched Cook
drawing thin lines across
the last sea's uncut book
is my own certain loss;

as too is having come late,
the other side of the dark
from that bearded, sedate
Hargrave of Stanwell Park,
and so to have missed, some bright
morning, in the salty, stiff
north-easter, a crank with a kite—
steadied above the cliff.

Beginnings once known
are lost. Perpetual day,
wheeling, has grown
each year further away
from the original strength
of any action or mind
used, and at length
fallen behind.

One might give much
to bring to the hand
for sight and touch
cities under the sand
and to talk and trade
with the plain folk met
could we walk with the first who made
an alphabet.

But more than to look back
we choose this day's concern
with everything in the track,
and would give most to learn
outcomes of all we found
and what next builds to the stars.
I regret I shall not be around
to stand on Mars.

Height

PINE-TREE, MADELINE STREET

Boughs of this pine are spokes that spread,
level, from hubs of stacked-up wheels
or rungs of a ladder height here scales
to infinity's outset overhead;
and either view of them blends the truth
in shapes reality doles to the eye
with mind's wonder which follows both
to the spire's point that stabs the sky.

Childhood observed of tree-tops
overlooking it through slow stir
of leafy sun, that, roused, they were
flails that would thrash to thunderclaps
and gale fury the air they fanned.

[Not victims were they, . . .

Not victims were they, beaten and bowed,
but pliant scourges that whipped the wind
and ripped sky-fabric to rags of cloud.

This was not wholly illusion. Fact,
for use, is in part the guise it wears
where sight watches and thought stares
and self and solidity interact—
as now, where height by warrant of
nods in the blue from this great pine
climbs growth to the limitless, above
summits of the world that has been mine.

JAMES PICOT

For it was Early Summer

Madelaine came running up the stair . . .

Not where the surf breaks,
                                    not in the glare, but under,
Anemones were warm in their green chamber . . .
Is the leaf a tendril or a finger?

Shades a delicious pool this coolibah . . .
Brown serpents mated in the mown alfalfa.

A jacaranda many jacarandas
Rocked lightly to the asphalt, all in purple.
Cradle-clothes, beside a camphor-laurel.

That Ayrshire in a brown and silver paddock
Ran away, in the grey and russet paddock . . .
When we tried to coax her, did we hoax her?

And birds? Their many notes trouble my spelling
With ecstasy: the dove,
Intolerably mellow;
Call, fall, trill, whistle, water-tumble telling
Love . . . to his fellow.

And Madelaine . . . running up the stair . . .
Racket and dress, brown face, became her hair!

CLIVE TURNBULL

Lost Love

Mr Todd is maudlin now—
clutches lapels and goggles up
at looming faces, glassy eyed.
Turbid sorrow fills his cup.

'She was a wunnerful woman,' says
Mr Todd, and hiccups, 'Chrise!
Boy, but how she fell for me . . .
Gawd, I tell yer, she was nice.'

Salty tears are Mr Todd's,
seeking lost love. But Mr Browne
is growing bored. He turns away,
tosses the pint of Foster's down.

'Ar, I tell yer': Mr Todd.
Comrade, look not on the west,
'Ar, I tell yer, she was nice . . .'
'Twill have the heart out of your breast.

41

Australia

A Nation of trees, drab green and desolate grey
In the field uniform of modern wars,
Darkens her hills, those endless, outstretched paws
Of Sphinx demolished or stone lion worn away.

They call her a young country, but they lie:
She is the last of lands, the emptiest,
A woman beyond her change of life, a breast
Still tender but within the womb is dry.

Without songs, architecture, history:
The emotions and superstitions of younger lands,
Her rivers of water drown among inland sands,
The river of her immense stupidity

Floods her monotonous tribes from Cairns to Perth.
In them at last the ultimate men arrive
Whose boast is not: 'we live' but 'we survive',
A type who will inhabit the dying earth.

And her five cities, like five teeming sores,
Each drains her: a vast parasite robber-state
Where second-hand Europeans pullulate
Timidly on the edge of alien shores.

Yet there are some like me turn gladly home
From the lush jungle of modern thought, to find
The Arabian desert of the human mind,
Hoping, if still from the deserts the prophets come,

Such savage and scarlet as no green hills dare
Springs in that waste, some spirit which escapes
The learned doubt, the chatter of cultured apes
Which is called civilization over there.

A. D. HOPE

Ascent into Hell

Little Henry, too, had a great notion of singing
HISTORY OF THE FAIRCHILD FAMILY

I, too, at the mid-point, in a well-lit wood
Of second-rate purpose and mediocre success,
Explore in dreams the never-never of childhood,
Groping in daylight for the key of darkness;

Revisit, among the morning archipelagoes,
Tasmania, my receding childish island;
Unchanged my prehistoric flora grows
Within me, marsupial territories extend:

There is the land-locked valley and the river,
The Western Tiers make distance an emotion,
The gum trees roar in the gale, the poplars shiver
At twilight, the church pines imitate an ocean.

There, in the clear night, still I listen, waking
To a crunch of sulky wheels on the distant road;
The marsh of stars reflects a starry croaking;
I hear in the pillow the sobbing of my blood

As the panic of unknown footsteps marching nearer,
Till the door opens, the inner world of panic
Nightmares that woke me to unawakening terror
Birthward resume their still inscrutable traffic.

Memory no more the backward, solid continent,
From island to island of despairing dream
I follow the dwindling soul in its ascent;
The bayonets and the pickelhauben gleam

Among the leaves, as, in the poplar tree,
They find him hiding. With an axe he stands
Above the German soldiers, hopelessly
Chopping the fingers from the climbing hands.

[Or, in the well-known . . .

Or, in the well-known house, a secret door
Opens on empty rooms from which a stair
Leads down to a grey, dusty corridor,
Room after room, ominous, still and bare.

He cannot turn back, a lurking horror beckons
Round the next corner, beyond each further door.
Sweating with nameless anguish then he wakens;
Finds the familiar walls blank as before.

Chased by wild bulls, his legs stick fast with terror.
He reaches the fence at last—the fence falls flat.
Choking, he runs, the trees he climbs will totter.
Or the cruel horns, like telescopes, shoot out.

At his fourth year the waking life turns inward.
Here on his Easter Island the stone faces
Rear meaningless monuments of hate and dread.
Dreamlike within the dream real names and places

Survive. His mother comforts him with her body
Against the nightmare of the lions and tigers.
Again he is standing in his father's study
Lying about his lie, is whipped, and hears

His scream of outrage, valid to this day.
In bed, he fingers his stump of sex, invents
How he took off his clothes and ran away,
Slit up his belly with various instruments;

To brood on this was a deep abdominal joy
Still recognized as a feeling at the core
Of love—and the last genuine memory
Is singing 'Jesus Loves Me'—then, no more!

Beyond is a lost country and in vain
I enter that mysterious territory.
Lit by faint hints of memory lies the plain
Where from its Null took shape this conscious I

Which backward scans the dark—But at my side
The unrecognized Other Voice speaks in my ear,
The voice of my fear, the voice of my unseen guide;
'Who are we, stranger? What are we doing here?'

And through the uncertain gloom, sudden I see
Beyond remembered time the imagined entry,
The enormous Birth-gate whispering, *'per me,
per me si va tra la perduta gente.'*

Imperial Adam

Imperial Adam, naked in the dew,
Felt his brown flanks and found the rib was gone.
Puzzled he turned and saw where, two and two,
The mighty spoor of Jahweh marked the lawn.

Then he remembered through mysterious sleep
The surgeon fingers probing at the bone,
The voice so far away, so rich and deep:
'It is not good for him to live alone.'

Turning once more he found Man's counterpart
In tender parody breathing at his side.
He knew her at first sight, he knew by heart
Her allegory of sense unsatisfied.

The pawpaw drooped its golden breasts above
Less generous than the honey of her flesh;
The innocent sunlight showed the place of love;
The dew on its dark hairs winked crisp and fresh.

This plump gourd severed from his virile root,
She promised on the turf of Paradise
Delicious pulp of the forbidden fruit;
Sly as the snake she loosed her sinuous thighs,

[And, waking, . . .

45

And waking, smiled up at him from the grass;
Her breasts rose softly and he heard her sigh—
From all the beasts whose pleasant task it was
In Eden to increase and multiply

Adam had learned the jolly deed of kind:
He took her in his arms and there and then,
Like the clean beasts, embracing from behind,
Began in joy to found the breed of men.

Then from the spurt of seed within her broke
Her terrible and triumphant female cry,
Split upward by the sexual lightning stroke.
It was the beasts now who stood watching by:

The gravid elephant, the calving hind,
The breeding bitch, the she-ape big with young
Were the first gentle midwives of mankind;
The teeming lioness rasped her with her tongue;

The proud vicuña nuzzled her as she slept
Lax on the grass; and Adam watching too
Saw how her dumb breasts at their ripening wept,
The great pod of her belly swelled and grew,

And saw its water break, and saw, in fear,
Its quaking muscles in the act of birth,
Between her legs a pigmy face appear,
And the first murderer lay upon the earth.

The Double Looking Glass

See how she strips her lily for the sun:
The silk shrieks upward from her wading feet;
Down through the pool her wavering echoes run;
Candour with candour, shade and substance meet.

A. D. HOPE

From where a wet meniscus rings the shin
The crisp air shivers up her glowing thighs,
Swells round a noble haunch and whispers in
The dimple of her belly . . . Surely eyes

Lurk in the laurels, where each leafy nest
Darts its quick bird-glance through the shifting screen.
. . . Yawn of the oxter, lift of liquid breast
Splinter their white shafts through our envious green

Where thuds this rage of double double hearts.
. . . My foolish fear refracts a foolish dream.
Here all things have imagined counterparts:
A dragon-fly dim-darting in the stream

Follows and watches with enormous eyes
His blue narcissus glitter in the air.
The flesh reverberates its own surprise
And startles at the act which makes it bare.

Laced with quick air and vibrant to the light,
Now my whole animal breathes and knows its place
In the great web of being, and its right;
The mind learns ease again, the heart finds grace.

I am as all things living. Man alone
Cowers from his world in clothes and cannot guess
How earth and water, branch and beast and stone
Speak to the naked in their nakedness.

. . . A silver rising of her arms, that share
Their pure and slender crescent with the pool
Plunders the braided treasure of her hair.
Loosed from their coils uncrowning falls the full

Cascade of tresses whispering down her flanks,
And idly now she wades a step, and stays
To watch the ripples widen to the banks
And lapse in mossy coves and rushy bays.

[Look with what bliss . . .

Look with what bliss of motion now she turns
And seats herself upon a sunny ledge,
Leans back, and drowsing dazzles, basking burns.
Susannah! . . . What hiss, what rustle in the sedge;

What fierce susurrus shifts from bush to bush?
. . . Susannah! Susannah, Susannah! . . . Foolish heart,
It was your own pulse lisping in a hush
So deep, I hear the water-beetle dart

And trace from bank to bank his skein of light,
So still the sibilance of a breaking bud
Speaks to the sense; the hairy bee in flight
Booms a brute chord of danger in my blood.

What danger though? The garden wall is high
And bolted and secure the garden door;
The bee, bold ravisher, will pass me by
And does not seek my honey for his store;

The speckled hawk in heaven, wheeling slow
Searches the tufts of grass for other prey;
Safe in their sunny banks the lilies grow,
Secure from rough hands for another day.

Alert and brisk, even the hurrying ant
Courses these breathing ranges unafraid.
The fig-tree, leaning with its leaves aslant,
Touches me with broad hands of harmless shade.

And if the urgent pulses of the sun
Quicken my own with a voluptuous heat,
They warm me only as they warm the stone
Or the thin liquid paddling round my feet.

My garden holds me like its private dream,
A secret pleasure, guarded and apart.
Now as I lean above the pool I seem
The image of my image in its heart.

In that inverted world a scarlet fish
Drifts through the trees and swims into the sky,
So in the contemplative mind a wish
Drifts through its mirror of eternity.

A mirror for man's images of love
The nakedness of woman is a pool
In which her own desires mount and move,
Alien, solitary, purposeful

Yet in this close were every leaf an eye,
In those green limbs the sap would mount as slow.
One with their life beneath an open sky,
I melt into the trance of time, I flow

Into the languid current of the day.
. . . The sunlight sliding on a breathing flank
Fades and returns again in tranquil play;
Her eyelids close; she sleeps upon the bank.

Now, now to wreak upon her Promised Land
The vengeance of the dry branch on the bud.
Who shall be first upon her? Who shall stand
To watch the dragon sink its fangs in blood?

Her ripeness taunts the ignominy of age;
Seethes in old loins with hate and lust alike.
Now in the plenitude of shame and rage
The rod of chastisement is reared to strike.

And now to take her drowsing; now to fall
With wild-fire on the cities of the plain;
Susannah! . . . Yet once more that hoarse faint call,
That rustle from the thicket comes again?

Ah, no! Some menace from the edge of sleep
Imposes its illusion on my ear.
Relax, return, Susannah; let the deep
Warm tide of noonday bear you; do not fear.

[But float once more . . .

But float once more on that delicious stream.
Suppose some lover watches from the grove;
Suppose, only suppose, those glints, the gleam
Of eyes; the eyes of a young man in love.

Shall I prolong this fancy, now the sense
Impels, the hour invites? Shall I not own
Such thoughts as women find to recompense
Their hidden lives when secret and alone?

Surprise the stranger in the heart, some strong
Young lion of the rocks who found his path
By night, and now he crouches all day long
Beside the pool to see me at my bath.

He would be there, a melancholy shade
Caught in the ambush of his reckless joy,
Afraid to stir for fear I call, afraid
In one unguarded moment to destroy

At once the lover and the thing he loves.
Who should he be? I cannot guess; but such
As desperate hope or lonelier passion moves
To tempt his fate so far, to dare so much;

Who having seen me only by the way,
Or having spoken with me once by chance,
Fills all his nights with longing, and the day
With schemes whose triumph is a casual glance.

Possessed by what he never can possess,
He forms his wild design and ventures all
Only to see me in my nakedness
And lurk and tremble by the garden wall.

He lives but in my dream. I need repel
No dream for I may end it when I please;
And I may dream myself in love as well
As dream my lover in the summer trees,

Suppose myself desired, suppose desire,
Summon that wild enchantment of the mind,
Kindle my fire at his imagined fire,
Pity his love and call him and be kind.

Now think he comes, and I shall lie as still
As limpid waters that reflect their sun,
And let him lie between my breasts and fill
My loins with thunder till the dream be done.

The kisses of my mouth are his; he lies
And feeds among the lilies, his brown knees
Divide the white embraces of my thighs.
Wake not my love nor stir him till he please,

For now his craft has passed the straits and now
Into my shoreless sea he drives alone.
Islands of spice await his happy prow
And fabulous deeps support and bear him on.

He rides the mounting surge, he feels the wide
Horizon draw him onward mile by mile;
The reeling sky, the dark rejoicing tide
Lead him at last to this mysterious isle.

In ancient woods that murmur with the sea,
He finds once more the garden and the pool.
And there a man who is and is not he
Basks on the sunny margin in the full

Noon of another and a timeless sky,
And dreams but never hopes to have his love;
And there the woman who is also I
Watches him from the hollow of the grove;

Till naked from the leaves she steals and bends
Above his sleep and wakes him with her breast
And now the vision begins, the voyage ends,
And the great phoenix blazes in his nest.

[. . . Ah, God of Israel, . . .

. . . Ah, God of Israel, even though alone,
We take her with a lover, in the flush
Of her desires. SUSANNAH! . . . I am undone!
What beards, what bald heads burst now from the bush!

In Memoriam: Gertrud Kolmar, 1943

Immer sind wir Blaubarts Frauen.

Whistling past this cemetery in the dark
Where most of your generation lie interred,
I think of Francis Bacon's *jeu d'esprit*:
'Kings are God's playfellows.' The great bone-park
Chuckles and rattles as if the dead had heard.
'Kings play at dangerous games.' They all agree,

We are proof that kings play a *very* dangerous game.
In a match against God, someone is bound to get hurt!
What was He doing, the morning they took you away,
For having a loving heart and a Jewish name,
While a king with a swastika badge on a brown shirt
Captained the opposite team and called the play?

Where was He, too, that night you mused in the dark,
Dog-tired, half-starved, the Terror just closing round,
Taking incredible comfort from St Just's joke:
'Men perish that God may live'? Did His Covenant Ark
Go before you to Auschwitz, his ram's-horn sound
Till the gas-chambers of Jericho breached and broke?

When they knocked you down and a jackboot kicked in your
     teeth,
Did you sing with Job: 'Though He slay me, yet will I trust'?
Or did you remember St Just and the poem you made,
That gay, that terrible poem confronting death:
'We have always been Bluebeard's wives; we always must!'?
That was your answer to God and games he played.

A. D. HOPE

We were all contracted, but we discovered instead
Once married that God was Bluebeard after all.
He had left on a journey, trusting us with a Key
To his universe. Alone in His double bed,
We wondered about that cupboard in the hall,
A forbidden closet, like the forbidden tree.

He had kissed us with lips that curved like scimitars,
Blood-red they smiled out of that blue-black beard.
The huge male bush hung over us like a threat;
Yet we knew we loved and were loved. The universe
Rang with His power and His love. When He disappeared
The Key was our comfort, His kiss a sign that He would not forget.

For love was our shield; love was our talisman;
Love was our guide the day we decided to use the Key.
So we crept to His closet door and opened it just a crack;
And there we saw clearly the whole condition of man.
Now we know the meaning of Bluebeard's love, and we
Quake in His castle of dread—pray that he will not come back.

But to whom do we pray? There is nobody else to hear.
Bluebeard is bound to return; He has heard our prayer.
He will come loving and smiling; ask for that blood-spotted key
While we cower in the bed of despair, that last, lost outpost of fear.
But you, you alone will stand up; you will teach us to dare;
You will teach us that calm at the worst, when the spirit goes free.

Whistling past your cemetery in the black
Storm of our century of hate and dread,
I, who have lived in shelter all of my days,
Bring you, before the Lord of the Keys gets back,
Word from all those still doomed to those who are already dead,
Those able to recognize all and yet still able to praise.

Stand back now, Azrael: I have a few moments yet.
You can have this carcass when I have had my say.
Yet what can I say for her, who said nothing at all
But dressed for her death like a bride: who paid the debt
Of the ancient doom of her race without dismay;
Who went to that doom as though to a festival?

All we can do, perhaps, is not to forget.

(Bluebeard is back! I have heard his step in the hall.)

RONALD McCUAIG

The Commercial Traveller's Wife

I'm living with a commercial traveller.
He's away, most of the time.
Most I see of him's his wife; as for her:
I'm just home from a show,
And there I am undressing, in my shirt.
I hear midnight chime,
And up flares the curtain at the window.
The door's opened. It's Gert—
That's the wife. Her hair's hanging down.
She's only got her nightgown
Blowing up against her in the wind.
She's fat, and getting fatter.
I said, 'What's the matter?'
'Jack,' she said, 'now's your chance.'
'What chance?' I said. 'You out of your mind?'
She goes over to the bed.
I grab my pants.
'That's enough of that,' I said. 'Now go on; you get out.'
'But Jack,' she said, 'don't you love me?'
'I don't know what you're talking about,'
I said. 'Besides, Jim—
  What about him?'
'Yes; Jim,' she said; 'there's always Jim, but he's
Always away. And you don't know
What it's like. I can't stand it. And anyhow,
Jack, don't you want me?'
                              'Oh, don't be an ass',
I said. 'Look at yourself in the glass.'
She faced the mirror where she stood
And sort of stiffened there.
Her eyes went still as knots in a bit of wood,
And it all seemed to sigh out of her:
'All right,' she said. 'All right, all right, good night',
As though she didn't know if I heard,
And shuffled out without another word.

Well, I was tired. I went to bed and slept.
In the morning
I thought I'd dreamt the whole thing,
But, at breakfast, I could have wept:
Poor Gert, clattering the dishes
With a dead sort of face
Like a fish's.
I'll have to get a new place.
I'm going out today to have a look.
Trouble is, she's a marvellous cook.

Au Tombeau de mon père

I went on Friday afternoons
Among the knives and forks and spoons
Where mounted grindstones flanked the floor
To my father's office door.

So serious a man was he,
The Buyer for the Cutlery . . .
I found him sketching lamps from stock
In his big stock-records book,

And when he turned the page to me:
'Not bad for an old codger, eh?'
I thought this frivolous in him,
Preferring what he said to them:

They wanted reparations paid
In German gold and not in trade,
But he rebuked such attitudes:
'You'll have to take it out in goods.'

And what they did in time was just.
He said, what he had said they must:
If Time had any end in sight
It was, to prove my father right.

[The evening came, . . .

The evening came, and changed him coats,
Produced a rag and rubbed his boots,
And then a mirror and a brush
And smoothed his beard and his moustache;

A sign for blinds outside to fall
On shelves and showcases, and all
Their hammers, chisels, planes and spades,
And pocket-knives with seven blades.

Then, in the lift, the patted back:
'He's growing like you, Mr Mac!'
(The hearty voices thus implied
A reason for our mutual pride.)

And so the front-door roundabout
Gathered us in and swept us out
To sausage, tea in separate pots,
And jellies crowned with creamy clots.

And once he took me on to a
Recital, to hear Seidel play,
And Hutchens spanked the piano-bass,
Never looking where it was.

When I got home I practised this,
But somehow always seemed to miss,
And my cigar-box violin,
After Seidel's, sounded thin.

And once he took me to a bill
Of sporadic vaudeville.
A man and woman held the stage;
She sneered in simulated rage,

And when he made a shrewd reply
He'd lift his oval shirt-front high
And slap his bare and hairy chest
To celebrate his raucous jest.

Then, as the shout of joy ensued,
Uniting mime and multitude,
And mine rang out an octave higher,
A boy-soprano's in that choir,

My father's smile was half unease,
Half pleasure in his power to please:
'Try not to laugh so loudly, Ron;
Those women think you're catching on.'

But far more often it was to
The School of Arts we used to go;
Up the dusty stairway's gloom,
Through the musty reading-room

And out to a veranda-seat
Overlooking Hunter Street.
There in the dark my father sat,
Pipe in mouth, to meditate.

A cake-shop glowed across the way
With a rainbow-cake display;
I never saw its keeper there,
And never saw a customer,

And yet there was activity
High in the south-western sky:
A bottle flashing on a sign
Advertising someone's wine.

So, as my father thought and thought
(Considering lines of saws he'd bought,
Or, silence both his church and club,
Feeling close to Nature's hub,

Or maybe merely practising
Never saying anything,
Since he could go, when deeply stirred,
Months, at home, without a word,

[Or pondering the indignity . . .

Or pondering the indignity
Of having to put up with me),
I contemplated, half awake,
The flashing wine, the glowing cake:

The wine that no one can decant,
And the cake we didn't want:
As Mr Blake's Redeemer said,
'This the wine, and this the bread.'

ELIZABETH RIDDELL

from *Country Tunes*

As I went out to walk
Beside the river flowing
I saw what I'd not hoped to see:
A black man washing a white horse.
That's how the world was going.

He washed the horse's tail
And plaited it with yellow.
The wild west show had come to town,
That's how I saw the high white horse
And the brave black fellow.

The wild hawks flew above the smoke,
Above the river flowing;
The drunken cowboy stumbled past
And his long legs without his will
Took him where he was going.

I saw his eyes of bitter blue
Who crossed my path unknowing,
Who would leap over my head that night,
Over the tent-pole, over the stars,
Over the river flowing.

I never hope to see again
The white horse decked in yellow,
The horse, the hawks, the river in flood,
The cowboy's eyes of bitter blue
Or the brave black fellow.

Space

Columbus looks towards the New World,
the sea is flat and nothing breaks the rim
of the world's disc;
he takes the sphere with him.

Day into night the same, the only change
the living variation at the core
of this man's universe;
and silent on the silver ship he broods.

Red gouts of weed, and skimming fish, to crack
the stupefying emptiness of sea;
night, and the unimpassioned gaze of stars . . .

And God be praised for the compass, oaths
bawled in the fo'c'sle,
broken heads and wine,
song and guitars,

the tramp of boots,
the wash and whip of brine.

Black Stockman

We talked about tobacco and the difficulties of getting it,
Quilp smoking an old black pipe,
Sucking at the ashes of ashes.
I gave him two cigarettes and his well-being broke into blossom
Just like a wrinkled old gum putting a white head
High into a singing cloud of bees.
'This is good tobacco,' he said.

[The horse's head . . .

The horse's head drooped lower and lower,
Flies pitched on the lids of his closed eyes and walked
Bravely round the inside of the bit-ring and off
On to the white-flecked lips. His tail hung thin,
Listless as a branch of leaves,
Paper-bark leaves above a billabong.

And we talked about cattle; we talked . . . But I
Lived in a long hiatus filled with a dreaming, seeing,
As eyes wandered, cows
Ankle-deep in black mud, reaching out
Long necks towards the soupy water, saw
The last limp leaves of dying lilies,
And a rotting blossom,

Talking to Quilp,
Talking to Quilp at the tail of a sleepy herd.

Traffic

Traffic up and down the coast all day
even if it's only a solitary gull
plodding into the wind. Three times
companies of birds went up the highway
travelling fast, very close to the waves
and flying line abreast, no leader,
going northward in a hurry, more like a long
brown ribbon fluttering than anything else.

Now we have a gull again, and the road otherwise empty,
unless you call the rain-squall far out there
on the horizon, standing on stilts, a traveller.
No fog-army in sight yet marching from the south.
The grey armies of fog and mist that invade the north
are Manco's soldiers on an Inca road
or ghosts of legions of Rome, bent forward,
loping along in double time.

WILLIAM HART-SMITH

The images, you may say, are far-fetched;
but that's what idleness does, enforced stillness.
I am fetched up here at a windowpane, with a view of the
    coast—
It's the porpoises I'm waiting for. I'll catch them this time.
Planes are important personages. They travel
with a rumble of conversation. Cloud-shadows
make a moving pattern of purple reefs
exposed to sight by the sun.

Even the waves are travellers because they break
shoreward at a tangent. That drowned log
won't come ashore anywhere in sight; some beachcomber
beyond the headland may have it and drag it home—
There they are! The porpoises! My favourite travellers.
They seem to stitch the grey-green sea
with a long running-stitch of some kind of
glistening black cotton, silk or sheen.

ROLAND ROBINSON

I had no Human Speech

I had no human speech. I heard
the quail-thrush cry out of the stones
and cry again its crystal word
out of the mountains' crumbling bones.

I had no human word, beyond
all words I knew the rush of ash-
grey wings that gloomed, with one respond,
storm-grey, to swerve with crimson flash.

[The speech that . . .

The speech that silence shapes but keeps:
a ruin and the writhe of thin
ghost-gums against their rain-blue deeps
of night and ranges I drank in.

I lived where mountains moved and stood
round me; I saw their natures change,
deepen and fire from mood to mood,
and found the kingfisher-blue range,

and found, where huge dark heliotrope
shadows pied a range's power,
mauve-purple at the foothills' slope,
the parakelia, the desert flower.

Yet, human, with unresting thought
tormented turned away from these
presences, from converse sought
with deserts, flowers, stones and trees.

The Myth and the Mountain

Look at that mountain Jalgumbun standing up.
Look how it goes straight up on all its sides.
No man can climb that mountain. Look at its head.
Look now through the mist, covered with trees.
I worked with Phinney McPherson the surveyor
right along this range, and when we come
to Jalgumbun, he says to me, 'Now Eustan,
let me see them steps you say are cut
out in this mountain.' And as I pointed out
them steps, he stood there, writing down
the story of the mountain that I told him.

That mountain Jalgumbun was once a tree.
A man went after honey in that tree.

He climbed up with the vine-rope round himself
and round the tree. And as he climbed he cut
out footholds with his stone-axe. And his wives
were waiting in the forest down below.
'Where are you?' they called out. And he called back,
'I'm chopping out the honey.' Then these women
wanted to come up closer, but again
the man sang out, 'No, wait there where you are.'
and went on chopping, chopping out the honey.
At last he called out, 'Here it is' and rolled
the piece of wood with all the honey in it
down to the butt and big roots of the tree.
They sat down in their camp and ate the honey,
and travelled then away out on the range.

That night there was no moon. The women looked
out into the night and spoke together,
'Oh, look, what is that "something" over there?'
'Oh, it is like a shadow . . .' 'See, that "something"
over there is blocking out the stars.'
And in the morning when they woke and looked
out, from the ranges where they'd camped, they saw
the mountain that was never there before,
Jalgumbun standing up against the sky.

Well, there's a tree called Jalgumbun that grows
here in the ranges. It has real soft skin.
The fellers from the mill at Urbenville
come with their tractors, axes and their gear,
and fell and lop them trees and drag them now
out from the ranges of their native home.

The Bone

I have a bone and all dogs chase me.
I flee with ears like cherubs' wings on glee's
shoulders; so fast my feet pace past
on a wizard's whirr and the dogs string
behind me like a comet's tail. I
have a message and everybody
wishes to halt the messenger charged
to effect swift delivery.
I will not drop the bone at the feet of
you, master. The chase continues with me
in possession. No dog bothers to
count the nine points. The chase continues.
Until I drop the bone, contention
will divide the pack. I'll be threatened
but known as the dog that stole the bone
a head's lead from the mongrel horde. If
I am caught I shall race on the flanks
of another hound. Nobody will
carry the bone to his threshold to crunch.
Too many contend to deliver the
message which hasn't been savoured by
anybody except the wind. Keep up
or you'll not stand a dog's chance. Cliches
will hinder you. You will forget the chase
which is an important link in the
chain of events. Dogfights divert
those hounds that have fallen behind the
pack. A cherub's wings favour the scroll
tied with ribbon and sealed with a prophet's
kiss. All is anonymous as a bone
filched from a prophet's tomb by feral
beasts. It is white. I have it, cannot
stop to appraise it. The chase is all
that assures me of its merit.

KENNETH MACKENZIE

The Moonlit Doorway

The peacock-eye of the half-moon long since up;
the peacock-blue of the iridescent sky
moonlit to starless pallor; the scream of peacocks
across the bay from here mock night together
outside my windows—a wild, gritty scorn,
a jeer at memory, a blue-lit laughter
at man and me.
    Once, though, there was a doorway
set full of night and this same genial pallor
of moon-made sky-magic. Memory
does not give jeer for jeer. Memory's faithful
and so am I to memory—even tonight
when the imperial birds across the bay
scream out their scornful warning through the light
of blue darkness: 'She was white and golden
in that dark room the moonlight entered no more.
She was a pale woman lying there
whom you have never seen, whom you have known
well at night only—never well by day.'
And that mad scream through the doorway of my windows,
though less with distance, still cries out 'Beware.'
Beware of you, it says, your man's fallibility
in keeping faith. Beware of moons and midnights
lest the white body of the beloved suffer
a sad sky-change, and through that moonlit doorway
pass headlong into the hell of discontent,
the double hell of conscience and of scorn,
the final hell of hate. Beware, beware . . .
    Of what I say. Of my heart? Of my mind?
Of the dark entry of this blood and flesh
into that younger and more innocent
flesh and blood, when the night was not far worn?
And I say, this was my fortune and delight,
and my long dreamed yet long withheld desire—
but more yet: my momentary destiny

                    [that dream should harden . . .

that dream should harden into softest flesh
which, melting to the tongue, almost returns
to dream. This was my fortune, that her breasts
should stand upright and for an hour or more
tell me this body warmed and tensed and turned
with love to mine. This was my fine reward
for nothing more than kisses and caresses—
that in some hour or two there should have been
utter forgetfulness of me and life
in the profundity of face-to-face
against a doorway full of the moonlit sky,
silence, solitude, and she and I
alone and together.
    Against the moonlit doorway is a tree,
flowered with a sparse but vigorous red by day
and black as a groping hand's lean skeleton
at night, when the moon's high. As I lay looking
I thought you had flown into it like a bird,
my child, my darling, silent and solitary
and watchful of the peacock treachery
of night, like a wary bird above the pool
of green lawn and new coming-together,
green knowledge and new understanding,
question, request, confession, answer, silence
as still as water. Then you were there again
with laughter in your mouth (I could not see
your clear eyes laughing in that silken darkness)
and in your hands a sudden secret cunning
as the desire and the will were mixed into
the slow and speechless deed itself. The tree
clawed kindly at the opal of the sky
with its red talons, and your own hands
are a mile away from you in space; and you
are a mile away from me, in space and time
and in intention. I, the servitor,
the bolder yet more humble of us two
who so astonishingly lie together,
am here no longer; I am in your body,
and, as the tree grown out of earth is earth,
so am I you, and you are my protection
against the tempests of the hated surface.

And into you I shall dissolve at last
with a great falling crash and sigh, contented.
    With your cool graveness of a painted angel,
what do you think of, child, bedded in darkness
with your feet towards the peacock-coloured panel
of the open door? Just that the game is over?
Just that the night is cold and I am warm?
(This is what we were made for.) Just that the doorway
is beautiful in its silky moonlit splendour
slashed once with the dagger-sounds of a dog's barking
and once again with the unholy cry
of the royal birds impassioned by the night?
Tell me now—so long afterwards but so soon—
what you think lazily about, stretched here at ease
across my arm and shoulder and my heart.
Or yet—these are your own words—why should you speak?
I speak enough for both. My tongue's uncaged,
the padlock opened by a key of passion,
the door sprung wide, the wooing moon of love
luring it out and on, across the lawns,
down through the trees of your own silences
into the valley of your quiet body,
into the shadow of your lidded eyes,
between the moonlike mountains of your bosom,
through the whole world that's you, until it falls
silent, and with a sigh we almost sleep.

Through the tall moonlit doorway night looks in,
and once again the peacocks cry at us.

Two Trinities

Are you ready? soul said again
smiling deep in the dark
where mind and I live passionately
grain rasping across grain
in a strangled question-mark
—or so we have lived lately.

               [I looked through . . .

I looked through the hollow keyhole
at my wife not young any more
with my signature on her forehead
and her spirit hers and whole
unsigned by me—as before
we knew each other, and wed.

I looked at my grown daughter
cool and contained as a flower
whose bees I shall not be among—
vivid as white spring water
full of womanish power
like the first phrases of a song.

I looked at my son, and wept
in my mouth's cave to see
the seed ready for sowing
and the harvest unready to be reaped—
green fruit shocked from the tree,
the bird killed on the wing.

Well? soul said and I said,
Mind and I are at one
to go with you now—finally
joined now to be led—for our place here is gone:
we are not among those three.

Soul said, *Now come with me.*

1 June 1952

An Old Inmate

Joe Green Joe Green O how are you doing today?
I'm well, he said, and the bones of his head looked noble.
That night they wheeled Joe Green on a whisper away
but his voice rang on in the ward: I'm a terrible trouble
to all you girls. I make you work for your pay.
If I 'ad my way I'd see that they paid you double.

KENNETH MACKENZIE

Joe Green Joe Green for eighty-two years and more
you walked the earth of your grandad's farm down-river
where oranges bigger than suns grow back from the shore
in the dark straight groves. Your love for life was a fever
that polished your eye and glowed in your cheek the more
the more you aged and pulsed in your voice for ever.

Joe Green looked down on his worked-out hands with scorn
and tears of age and sickness and pride and wonder
lay on his yellow cheek where the grooves were worn
shallow and straight: but the scorn of his look was tender
like a lover's who hears reproaches meet to be borne
and his voice no more than echoed its outdoor thunder:

Gi' me the good old days and the old-time folk.
You don't find that sort now you clever young fellers.
Wireless motorbikes all this American talk
and the pitchers and atom-bombs. O' course it follers
soon you'll forget 'ow to read or think or walk—
and there won't be one o' you sleeps at night on your pillers!

Joe Green Joe Green let us hear what your grandad said
when you were a lad and the oranges not yet planted
on the deep soil where the dark wild children played
the land that Governor King himself had granted
fifteen decades ago that the Green men made
a mile-square Eden where nothing that lived there wanted.

Joe Green lay back and smiled at the western sun:
'Fear God and the women, boy,' was his only lesson,
'and love 'em—but on the 'ole just leave 'em alone,
the women specially.' Maybe I didn't listen
all of the time. A man ain't made of stone . . .
But I done my share of praying and fearing and kissing.

No. I 'ad no dad nor mum of me own—
not to remember—but still I'd a good upbringing.
The gran'ma raised thirty-two of us all alone
child and grandchild . . . Somewhere a bell goes ringing.
Steps and the shielded lanterns come and are gone.
The old voice rocks with laughter and tears and singing.

[Gi' me the good old days . . .

KENNETH MACKENZIE

Gi' me the good old days . . . Joe Green Joe Green
how are you doing tonight? Is it cold work dying?
Not 'alf so cold as some of the frosts I've seen
out Sackville way . . . The voice holds fast defying
sleep and silence, the whisper and the trifold screen
and the futile difficult sounds of his old girl's crying.

11 July 1953

DOUGLAS STEWART

Terra Australis

1
Captain Quiros and Mr William Lane,
Sailing some highway shunned by trading traffic
Where in the world's skull like a moonlit brain
Flashing and crinkling rolls the vast Pacific,

Approached each other zigzag, in confusion,
Lane from the west, the Spaniard from the east,
Their flickering canvas breaking the horizon
That shuts the dead off in a wall of mist.

'Three hundred years since I set out from Lima
And off Espiritu Santo lay down and wept
Because no faith in men, no truth in islands
And still unfound the shining continent slept;

'And swore upon the Cross to come again
Though fever, thirst and mutiny stalked the seas
And poison spiders spun their webs in Spain,
And did return, and sailed three centuries,

'Staring to see the golden headlands wade
And saw no sun, no land, but this wide circle
Where moonlight clots the waves with coils of weed
And hangs like silver moss on sail and tackle,

'Until I thought to trudge till time was done
With all except my purpose run to waste;
And now upon this ocean of the moon,
A shape, a shade, a ship, and from the west!'

2
'What ship?' 'The *Royal Tar*!' 'And whither bent?'
'I seek the new Australia.' 'I, too, stranger;
Terra Australis, the great continent
That I have sought three centuries and longer;

'And westward still it lies, God knows how far,
Like a great golden cloud, unknown, untouched,
Where men shall walk at last like spirits of fire
No more by oppression chained, by sin besmirched.'

'Westward there lies a desert where the crow
Feeds upon poor men's hearts and picks their eyes;
Eastward we flee from all that wrath and woe
And Paraguay shall yet be Paradise.'

'Eastward,' said Quiros, as *San Pedro* rolled,
High-pooped and round in the belly like a barrel,
'Men tear each other's entrails out for gold;
And even here I find that men will quarrel.'

'If you are Captain Quiros you are dead.'
'The report has reached me; so is William Lane.'
The dark ships rocked together in the weed
And Quiros stroked the beard upon his chin:

'We two have run this ocean through a sieve
And though our death is scarce to be believed
Seagulls and flying-fish were all it gave
And it may be we both have been deceived.'

3
'Alas, alas, I do remember now;
In Paradise I built a house of mud
And there were fools who could not milk a cow
And idle men who would not though they could.

'There were two hundred brothers sailed this ocean
To build a New Australia in the east
And trifles of money caused the first commotion
And one small cask of liquor caused the last.

'Some had strange insects bite them, some had lust,
For wifeless men will turn to native women,
Yet who could think a world would fall in dust
And old age dream of smoke and blood and cannon

'Because three men got drunk?' 'With Indian blood
And Spanish hate that jungle reeked to Heaven;
And yet I too came once, or thought I did,
To Terra Australis, my dear western haven,

'And broke my gallows up in scorn of violence,
Gave land and honours, each man had his wish,
Flew saints upon the rigging, played the clarions:
Yet many there were poisoned by a fish

'And more by doubt; and so deserted Torres
And sailed, my seamen's prisoner, back to Spain.'
There was a certain likeness in the stories
And Captain Quiros stared at William Lane.

4
Then 'Hoist the mainsail!' both the voyagers cried,
Recoiling each from each as from the devil;
'How do we know that we are truly dead
Or that the tales we tell may not be fable?

'Surely I only dreamed that one small bottle
Could blow up New Australia like a bomb?
A mutinous pilot I forebore to throttle
From Terra Australis send me demented home?

'The devil throws me up this Captain Quiros,
This William Lane, a phantom not yet born,
This Captain Quiros dead three hundred years,
To tempt me to disaster for his scorn—

'As if a blast of bony breath could wither
The trees and fountains shining in my mind,
Some traveller's tale, puffed out in moonlit weather,
Divert me from the land that I must find!

'Somewhere on earth that land of love and faith
In Labour's hands—the Virgin's—must exist,
And cannot lie behind, for there is death,
So where but in the west—but in the east?'

At that the sea of light began to dance
And plunged in sparkling brine each giddy brain;
The wind from Heaven blew both ways at once
And west went Captain Quiros, east went Lane.

B Flat

Sing softly, Muse, the Reverend Henry White
Who floats through time as lightly as a feather
Yet left one solitary gleam of light
Because he was the Selborne naturalist's brother

And told him once how on warm summer eves
When moonlight filled all Fyfield to the brim
And yearning owls were hooting to their loves
On church and barn and oak-tree's leafy limb

[He took a common . . .

He took a common half-a-crown pitch-pipe
Such as the masters used for harpsichords
And through the village trod with silent step
Measuring the notes of those melodious birds

And found that each one sang, or rather hooted,
Precisely in the measure of B flat.
And that is all that history has noted;
We know no more of Henry White than that.

So, softly, Muse, in harmony and conformity
Pipe up for him and all such gentle souls
Thus in the world's enormousness, enormity,
So interested in music and in owls;

For though we cannot claim his crumb of knowledge
Was worth much more than virtually nil
Nor hail him for vast enterprise or courage,
Yet in my mind I see him walking still

With eager ear beneath his clerical hat
Through Fyfield village sleeping dark and blind,
Oh surely as he piped his soft B flat
The most harmless, the most innocent of mankind.

The Snow-gum

It is the snow-gum silently,
In noon's blue and the silvery
Flowering of light on snow,
Performing its slow miracle
Where upon drift and icicle
Perfect lies its shadow.

DOUGLAS STEWART

Leaf upon leaf's fidelity,
The creamy trunk's solidity,
The full-grown curve of the crown,
It is the tree's perfection
Now shown in clear reflection
Like flakes of soft grey stone.

Out of the granite's eternity,
Out of the winters' long enmity,
Something is done on the snow;
And the silver light like ecstasy
Flows where the green tree perfectly
Curves to its perfect shadow.

The Silkworms

All their lives in a box! What generations,
What centuries of masters, not meaning to be cruel
But needing their labour, taught these creatures such patience
That now though sunlight strikes on the eye's dark jewel
Or moonlight breathes on the wing they do not stir
But like the ghosts of moths crouch silent there.

Look it's a child's toy! There is no lid even,
They can climb, they can fly, and the whole world's their tree;
But hush, they say in themselves, we are in prison.
There is no word to tell them that they are free,
And they are not; ancestral voices bind them
In dream too deep for wind or word to find them.

Even in the young, each like a little dragon
Ramping and green upon his mulberry leaf,
So full of life, it seems, the voice has spoken:
They hide where there is food, where they are safe,
And the voice whispers, 'Spin the cocoon,
Sleep, sleep, you shall be wrapped in me soon.'

[Now is their hour, . . .

75

DOUGLAS STEWART

Now is their hour, when they wake from that long swoon;
Their pale curved wings are marked in a pattern of leaves,
Shadowy for trees, white for the dance of the moon;
And when on summer nights the buddleia gives
Its nectar like lilac wine for insects mating
They drink its fragrance and shiver, impatient with waiting,

They stir, they think they will go. Then they remember
It was forbidden, forbidden, ever to go out;
The Hands are on guard outside like claps of thunder,
The ancestral voice says Don't, and they do not.
Still the night calls them to unimaginable bliss
But there is terror around them, the vast, the abyss,

And here is the tribe that they know, in their known place,
They are gentle and kind together, they are safe for ever,
And all shall be answered at last when they embrace.
White moth moves closer to moth, lover to lover.
There is that pang of joy on the edge of dying—
Their soft wings whirr, they dream that they are flying.

J. M. COUPER

Horace, Odes, 1, 5
SURFERS' PARADISE

What cheerful bastard
reeking of sun-tan
goes for you, Angela,
flat on the sand?

Just the old boy-friend
writing to ask you
who cops the hair-do,
coolest of bitches?

76

J. M. COUPER

My, but he's in for a
tough old time there,
tossing the seas of your
greedy libido.

Won't know it yet, though,
now he enjoys you,
always plain sailing,
so easy always.

Sucker, like all of us,
silly at the sight of
that dropping lee shore, your
sunsmitten bottom.

Here am I writing this
thankful tribute and
drying my wings like a
shag on a rock.

DAVID CAMPBELL

Men in Green

There were fifteen men in green,
Each with a tommy-gun,
Who leapt into my plane at dawn;
We rose to meet the sun.

We set our course towards the east
And climbed into the day
Till the ribbed jungle underneath
Like a giant fossil lay.

[We climbed towards . . .

DAVID CAMPBELL

We climbed towards the distant range
Where two white paws of cloud
Clutched at the shoulders of the pass;
The green men laughed aloud.

They did not fear the ape-like cloud
That climbed the mountain crest
And hung from twisted ropes of air
With thunder in its breast.

They did not fear the summer's sun
In whose hot centre lie
A hundred hissing cannon shells
For the unwatchful eye.

And when on Dobadura's field
We landed, each man raised
His thumb towards the open sky;
But to their right I gazed.

For fifteen men in jungle green
Rose from the kunai grass
And came towards the plane. My men
In silence watched them pass;
It seemed they looked upon themselves
In Time's prophetic glass.

Oh, there were some leaned on a stick
And some on stretchers lay,
But few walked on their own two feet
In the early green of day.

They had not feared the ape-like cloud
That climbed the mountain crest;
They had not feared the summer's sun
With bullets for their breast.

Their eyes were bright, their looks were dull,
Their skin had turned to clay.
Nature had met them in the night
And stalked them in the day.

And I think still of men in green
On the Soputa track
With fifteen spitting tommy-guns
To keep a jungle back.

Windy Gap

As I was going through Windy Gap
A hawk and a cloud hung over the map.

The land lay bare and the wind blew loud
And the hawk cried out from the heart of the cloud,

'Before I fold my wings in sleep
I'll pick the bones of your travelling sheep,

'For the leaves blow back and the wintry sun
Shows the tree's white skeleton.'

A magpie sat in the tree's high top
Singing a song on Windy Gap

That streamed far down to the plain below
Like a shaft of light from a high window.

From the bending tree he sang aloud,
And the sun shone out of the heart of the cloud

And it seemed to me as we travelled through
That my sheep were the notes that trumpet blew.

And so I sing this song of praise
For travelling sheep and blowing days.

DAVID CAMPBELL

Dear Maurice

Dear Maurice, Sure I understand,
You lost your bearings, like you told.
I'd not be reared here, on the land,
And doubt you. Nights are cruel cold
And fogs come sudden. Peaks are clear,
And the next turning, for my life
I'd not know man from fox or hare;—
And you were company for the wife.
While writing this, this minute, night,
Near twelve o'clock, against the pane
A moth came tapping in the light,
When snap! a nighthawk drops as plain
As day, and snuffs him.—This, of course,
Is by the way. Sincerely yours . . .

Mothers and Daughters

The cruel girls we loved
Are over forty,
Their subtle daughters
Have stolen their beauty;

And with a blue stare
Of cool surprise,
They mock their anxious mothers
With their mothers' eyes.

DAVID CAMPBELL

The Australian Dream

The doorbell buzzed. It was past three o'clock.
The steeple-of-Saint-Andrew's weathercock
Cried silently to darkness, and my head
Was bronze with claret as I rolled from bed
To ricochet from furniture. Light! Light
Blinded the stairs, the hatstand sprang upright,
I fumbled with the lock, and on the porch
Stood the Royal Family with a wavering torch.

'We hope,' the Queen said, 'we do not intrude.
The pubs were full, most of our subjects rude.
We came before our time. It seems the Queen's
Command brings only, "Tell the dead marines!"
We've come to you.' I must admit I'd half
Expected just this visit. With a laugh
That put them at their ease, I bowed my head.
'Your Majesty is most welcome here,' I said.
'My home is yours. There is a little bed
Downstairs, a boiler-room, might suit the Duke.'
He thanked me gravely for it and he took
Himself off with a wave. 'Then the Queen Mother?
She'd best bed down with you. There is no other
But my wide bed. I'll curl up in a chair.'
The Queen looked thoughtful. She brushed out her hair
And folded up *The Garter* on a pouf.
'Distress was the first commoner, and as proof
That queens bow to the times,' she said, 'we three
Shall share the double bed. Please follow me.'

I waited for the ladies to undress—
A sense of fitness, even in distress,
Is always with me. They had tucked away
Their state robes in the lowboy; gold crowns lay
Upon the bedside tables; ropes of pearls
Lassoed the plastic lampshade; their soft curls
Were spread out on the pillows and they smiled.

['Hop in,' . . .

DAVID CAMPBELL

'Hop in,' said the Queen Mother. In I piled
Between them to lie like a stick of wood.
I couldn't find a thing to say. My blood
Beat, but like rollers at the ebb of tide.
'I hope your Majesties sleep well,' I lied.
A hand touched mine and the Queen said, 'I am
Most grateful to you, Jock. Please call me Ma'am.'

J. S. MANIFOLD

The Tomb of
Lt. John Learmonth, A.I.F.

'At the end on Crete he took to the hills, and said he'd fight
it out with only a revolver. He was a great soldier.'. . .
                                        —One of his men in a letter.

This is not sorrow, this is work: I build
A cairn of words over a silent man,
My friend John Learmonth whom the Germans killed.

There was no word of hero in his plan;
Verse should have been his love and peace his trade,
But history turned him to a partisan.

Far from the battle as his bones are laid
Crete will remember him. Remember well,
Mountains of Crete, the Second Field Brigade!

Say Crete, and there is little more to tell
Of muddle tall as treachery, despair
And black defeat resounding like a bell;

But bring the magnifying focus near
And in contempt of muddle and defeat
The old heroic virtues still appear.

Australian blood where hot and icy meet
(James Hogg and Lermontov were of his kin)
Lie still and fertilise the fields of Crete.

*   *   *

Schoolboy, I watched his ballading begin:
Billy and bullocky and billabong,
Our properties of childhood, all were in.

I heard the air though not the undersong,
The fierceness and resolve; but all the same
They're the tradition, and tradition's strong.

Swagman and bushranger die hard, die game,
Die fighting, like that wild colonial boy—
Jack Dowling, says the ballad, was his name.

He also spun his pistol like a toy,
Turned to the hills like wolf or kangaroo,
And faced destruction with a bitter joy.

His freedom gave him nothing else to do
But set his back against his family tree
And fight the better for the fact he knew

He was as good as dead. Because the sea
Was closed and the air dark and the land lost,
'They'll never capture me alive', said he.

*   *   *

That's courage chemically pure, uncrossed
With sacrifice or duty or career,
Which counts and pays in ready coin the cost

[Of holding . . .

Of holding course. Armies are not its sphere
Where all's contrived to achieve its counterfeit;
It swears with discipline, it's volunteer.

I could as hardly make a moral fit
Around it as around a lightning flash.
There is no moral, that's the point of it,

No moral. But I'm glad of this panache
That sparkles, as from flint, from us and steel,
True to no crown nor presidential sash

Nor flag nor fame. Let others mourn and feel
He died for nothing: nothings have their place.
While thus the kind and civilised conceal

This spring of unsuspected inward grace
And look on death as equals, I am filled
With queer affection for the human race.

A Hat in the Ring

To Ann Coleman

N.   Verse? Writing verse? Dear man, are you insane?
        To think I used to think you had a brain!
        This is not Arcady; the days are gone
        When Phyllis babbled verse to Corydon.
        Wake up! Queen Anne is dead, and Pope as well.
        So's Burns, so's Keats, so's Byron . . .

M.   Go to hell.
        Talk to your friends or rollick in a stew,
        Go anywhere, but go. I've work to do.

J. S. MANIFOLD

N. You call it work? I call it waste of time
To brood and curse and mumble scraps of rhyme.
For what's to show? No publisher prevails
On press and populace to swell your sales.
Novels, I grant, and travel books are sound,
But verse will never bring you fifty pound:
Books may be published, bought and read, it's true,
But not in verse, and not by such as you.
What sort of thing's a poet when all's said?
A gutless creature with an empty head
Given to sandals, corduroys, and beard
And curious vices too from all I've heard.

M. Come off that tack, your case is inside out;
Poets make verse, not t'other way about.
Are you less Tory when a peer is found
Cheating th' Exchequer or the Underground?
Do you abandon business when you hear
The sentence passed upon a profiteer?
And yet you'd have me drop my own employs
Because Bombastes sleeps with little boys,
Christ, you're a fool!

N.   Maybe; it's not a crime.
But what's the use of verse at any time?

M. You use it all the time—to rest your brains
You pinch from Pope and mangle Gray's quatrains.
You sing the stuff at Christmas and New Year
And wallow in it when you're full of beer.
I've seen you moved to frenzy when you heard
A limerick rhyming on a bawdy word,
And weeping with emotion when they sing
At patriotic functions 'Save the King.'
You clap and cheer the man who knows by heart
'Eskimo Nell' and 'Lady Jane the Tart,'
And get more pleasure from them at a guess
Than from the films, the wireless, or the press.
It has been said and will be said again,
'The typewriter is mightier than the Bren';
Perhaps I have to emphasize for you
First, that it scans, and second, that it's true.

J. S. MANIFOLD

N. That's neat enough. But let them speak themselves,
Those pretty volumes standing on your shelves—
Those of the day, the ones who 'boldly cope
With modern problems'; who 'enlarge the scope
Of consciousness,' (I read the best reviews)—
Please let me see them do it; pick one; choose.

M. Delve where one may, the yield's about as good
As diamonds in clay or gold in mud:—
Here's the Apocalypse, so called, and there
That tough old pixy Walter de la Mare;
There Delphic Thomas rages on his stool,
There Gaffer Pound still acts the ageing fool
Ochred and peevish in his motley dress
Of Chinese proverbs, French and fractiousness;
Here's Blut-und-Boden Lawrence, here at hand
A. P. (for Pangloss) Herbert's ballads stand;
Here simple Spender in a place apart
Bares on his sleeve his haemophilic heart;
Dribble by drip the pinkish flow proceeds—
Oh, squeeze it, Mister Spender! Thar she bleeds!
Long since, a Sweet Young Thing, he staked his claim,
His vein a gusher proved, he rose to fame,
Postured in public with a nudist's smile.
Outbled a pig, outwept a crocodile;
First with the mode and duly quick to please
He spread like smut on crops or mites on cheese,
Till half the press submitted to his reign
And soft contagion ran through all their train.
Now in degenerate prose, not verse alone,
He rapes (as formerly he bayed) the moon;
Now, as a critic, shows for all to see
Shelley and Whitman were the same as he.
The passing years brought little change of plan—
The Sweet Young Thing became a Grand Old Man.
But as boloney, slice it where you will,
Remains boloney, pure boloney still,
So he continues and his constant theme
Is this unpleasant moist and sticky stream.
        So much for him. And here the rabble grows
Which must elucidate its verse in prose;
Those who were sad at school, and ever since

Have learnt no tactic but to weep and wince;
Those whose subconsciousnesses need spring cleaning
And those who Blunden round about a meaning;
Those whom this age disgusts and those it bores,
Who flee to childhood, Yoga, foreign shores . . .

N. You give me points enough.

M.   I give you none.
You ask for poets—take a look at one:
Right by your hand the single volume lies
Of one I knew courageous, strong and wise;
One of the few through all the years of shame
Who reconciled me to my English name,
Man-sized and tough and full of guts and pride
He lived and loved and fought like hell and died;
Cornford, who spoke like an exploding shell;
To mind and fingers and the heart as well;
Bare, bitter with the truth, not posed, not slick,
Here's verse that's more than good—it's bolshevik!

N. He was so young . . .

M.   You mean that by degrees
He might have mellowed into writing 'Trees'?
The Young! Hell's fire, as if an artist froze
And held a hundred years a single pose!
That style's the man has seldom been contested—
The self-styled Young are mentally arrested.
Well, I am not The Young, nor do I claim
To speak in theirs or any age's name.
Young I may be, but younger learnt my trade:
People are born, but poets must be made.
To earn his keep, a poet has to be
Himself, his age, and his society;
Not bawling run to Nature for relief,
Nor seal his ears and eyes with selfish grief,
Nor yet make self-expression all his goal,
Nor try too hard to save or lose his soul,
Not live in libraries but on the streets

[On equal terms with . . .

On equal terms with any man he meets.
I'd have him active, social, not apart,
Bold in his thought, proficient in his art,
Apt from his audience to accept his form,
Game to compose and eager to perform,
Close to his listeners—within shouting reach—
Alert to fit their mood with song or speech,
Quick on the draw and good at the guitar
As Lorca was . . .

N.   And you believe you are?

M. Not yet, but shall be one day, and meanwhile
I live my life and let it shape my style.
    If thus a poet live, you may depend
No self-important Book Club stands his friend,
No Fairy Ring surrounds his person, no
Art-smart suburban buys his book for show;
Unpraised, unscathed by broadcast or review,
He foils the Foyles and shames the devil too.
But—quote his works in pubs and none will jeer;
Declaimed on May Day he makes hundreds cheer,
Sung on the march, where parody, not thanks,
Greets pompous stuff, he unifies the ranks;
Drunks choose his silly songs, his limericks please—
And what's a pedant's praise compared to these?
Change names and places, such a man by turns
Is Henry Lawson, Lorca, Brecht, or Burns
Or becomes part of him the critics call
'Anon,' the greatest poet of them all.
    Personal fame derives from paltry means,
Is earned by gangsters, peers, and beauty queens;
Leave it to such. A decent verse will thrive
Uncumbered by an author dead or live,
While of our modern poets so polite
All know the names but few know what they write.
    In spite of all, good poems prosper still;
Where Reds foregather, there you'll hear Joe Hill;
Or ask the Army—plenty can repeat
With bitter relish 'Sixty Cubic Feet';
With 'Cucaracha' Villa rides again,
And Banjo fires Australia's fighting men.

(Don't quote the BBC to prove me wrong
Whose misconception of our battle song
Perverts the cadence, b——s up the time,
And adds to England's record one more crime.)
      No man exists but song can touch his mind
And make him proudly conscious of his kind.
You who consider song so slight and frail,
Tell me why Erich Mühsam went to gaol,
Or when Jack Donahue was safely hung
Why it was made a crime to have him sung.
Suppose—it's just as easy as it seems—
The paper shortage reaches the extremes;
Suppose no papers, or at most a sheet
Of Government news, no posters in the street,
No books for sale, and all the old destroyed:
Would poets then or prose men be employed?
What lives except the quick repeated rhyme?
And that's what did occur in Mayakovsky's time.
      Verse is the chain of words in which to bind
The things we wish most often brought to mind.
Think of an ore new-fossicked, sparse and crude;
Stamped out and minted it will buy your food,
Cajole a mistress, soften the police,
Raise a revolt, or win ignoble peace,
Corrupt or strengthen, sunder or rejoin;
Words are the quartz, but poetry's the coin.
      Guerilla words, the flying pasquinade,
The slogan-epigram's stiletto blade,
The loud Come-all-ye to a ballad air,
The declamation in the crowded square,
The spoken sonnet, eloquent and terse:
These are the proper marks for adult verse;
No job for 'wonder-children' but most fit
To show Invention, Eloquence and Wit.
And yield that best reward the poet needs—
To know his Words result in worthy Deeds.

N. Why then, you've worn me down, and I can see
From your expression that the drink's on me;
So prove your point and move me—to the bar—
With verse.

M.   Too easy. Reach me the guitar.

J. S. MANIFOLD

Fife Tune

for Sixth Platoon, 308th I.T.C.

One morning in spring
We marched from Devizes
All shapes and all sizes
Like beads on a string,
But yet with a swing
We trod the bluemetal
And full of high fettle
We started to sing.

She ran down the stair
A twelve-year-old darling
And laughing and calling
She tossed her bright hair;
Then silent to stare
At the men flowing past her—
There were all she could master
Adoring her there.

It's seldom I'll see
A sweeter or prettier;
I doubt we'll forget her
In two years or three,
And lucky he'll be
She takes for a lover
While we are far over
The treacherous sea.

Brother and Sisters

The road turned out to be a cul-de-sac;
stopped like a lost intention at the gate
and never crossed the mountains to the coast.
But they stayed on. Years grew like grass and leaves
across the half-erased and dubious track
until one day they knew the plans were lost,
the blue-print for the bridge was out of date,
and now their orchards never would be planted.
The saplings sprouted slyly; day by day
the bush moved one step nearer, wondering when.
The polished parlour grew distrait and haunted
where Millie, Lucy, John each night at ten
wound the gilt clock that leaked the year away.

The pianola—oh, listen to the mocking-bird—
wavers on Sundays and has lost a note.
The wrinkled ewes snatch pansies through the fence
and stare with shallow eyes into the garden
where Lucy shrivels waiting for a word,
and Millie's cameos loosen round her throat.
The bush comes near, the ranges grow immense.

Feeding the lambs deserted in early spring
Lucy looked up and saw the stockman's eye
telling her she was cracked and old.
                                    The wall
groans in the night and settles more awry.
O how they lie awake. Their thoughts go fluttering
from room to room like moths: 'Millie, are you awake?'
'Oh John, I have been dreaming.' 'Lucy, do you cry?'
—meet tentative as moths. Antennae stroke a wing.
'There is nothing to be afraid of. Nothing at all.'

JUDITH WRIGHT

South of My Days

South of my days' circle, part of my blood's country,
rises that tableland, high delicate outline
of bony slopes wincing under the winter,
low trees blue-leaved and olive, outcropping granite—
clean, lean, hungry country. The creek's leaf-silenced,
willow-choked, the slope a tangle of medlar and crabapple
branching over and under, blotched with a green lichen;
and the old cottage lurches in for shelter.

O cold the black-frost night. The walls draw in to the warmth
and the old roof cracks its joints; the slung kettle
hisses a leak on the fire. Hardly to be believed that summer
will turn up again some day in a wave of rambler roses,
thrust its hot face in here to tell another yarn—
a story old Dan can spin into a blanket against the winter.
Seventy years of stories he clutches round his bones.
Seventy summers are hived in him like old honey.

Droving that year, Charleville to the Hunter,
nineteen-one it was, and the drought beginning;
sixty head left at the McIntyre, the mud round them
hardened like iron; and the yellow boy died
in the sulky ahead with the gear, but the horse went on,
stopped at the Sandy Camp and waited in the evening.
It was the flies we seen first, swarming like bees.
Came to the Hunter, three hundred head of a thousand—
cruel to keep them alive—and the river was dust.

Or mustering up in the Bogongs in the autumn
when the blizzards came early. Brought them down; we
    brought them
down, what aren't there yet. Or driving for Cobb's on the run
up from Tamworth—Thunderbolt at the top of Hungry Hill,
and I give him a wink. I wouldn't wait long, Fred,
not if I was you; the troopers are just behind,
coming for that job at the Hillgrove. He went like a luny,
him on his big black horse.

Oh, they slide and they vanish
as he shuffles the years like a pack of conjuror's cards.
True or not, it's all the same; and the frost on the roof
cracks like a whip, and the back-log breaks into ash.
Wake, old man. This is winter, and the yarns are over.
No one is listening.
South of my days' circle
I know it dark against the stars, the high lean country
full of old stories that still go walking in my sleep.

Woman to Man

The eyeless labourer in the night,
the selfless, shapeless seed I hold,
builds for its resurrection day—
silent and swift and deep from sight
foresees the unimagined light.

This is no child with a child's face;
this has no name to name it by:
yet you and I have known it well.
This is our hunter and our chase,
the third who lay in our embrace.

This is the strength that your arm knows,
the arc of flesh that is my breast,
the precise crystals of our eyes.
This is the blood's wild tree that grows
the intricate and folded rose.

This is the maker and the made;
this is the question and reply;
the blind head butting at the dark,
the blaze of light along the blade.
Oh hold me, for I am afraid.

JUDITH WRIGHT

Train Journey

Glassed with cold sleep and dazzled by the moon,
out of the confused hammering dark of the train
I looked and saw under the moon's cold sheet
your delicate dry breasts, country that built my heart;

and the small trees on their uncoloured slope
like poetry moved, articulate and sharp
and purposeful under the great dry flight of air,
under the crosswise currents of wind and star.

Clench down your strength, box-tree and ironbark.
Break with your violent root the virgin rock.
Draw from the flying dark its breath of dew
till the unliving come to life in you.

Be over the blind rock a skin of sense,
under the barren height a slender dance . . .

I woke and saw the dark small trees that burn
suddenly into flowers more lovely than the white moon.

Extinct Birds

Charles Harpur in his journals long ago
(written in hope and love, and never printed)
recorded the birds of his time's forest—
birds long vanished with the fallen forest—
described in copperplate on unread pages.

The scarlet satin-bird, swung like a lamp in berries,
he watched in love, and then in hope described it.
There was a bird, blue, small, spangled like dew.
All now are vanished with the fallen forest.
And he, unloved, past hope, was buried,

who helped with proud stained hands to fell the forest,
and set those birds in love on unread pages;
yet thought himself immortal, being a poet.
And is he not immortal, where I found him,
in love and hope along his careful pages?—
the poet vanished, in the vanished forest,
among his brightly tinted extinct birds?

Some Words

UNLESS

Had a whole dream once
full of nothing else.

A bottomless pit,
eyes bulged out
across it,
neck stretched
over it.

A whole life I know of
fell into it
once;
and never came back.

THEREFORE

Three white lines
joining exactly,
all the angles
equal.

Inside it—
symmetrical
cross-legged,
one finger up,
expounding a simple fact
sits Nobody.

[A perfect confined . . .

JUDITH WRIGHT

A perfect confined space;
not one star
shines in.

ENOUGH

No use, we'll never catch it.
It's just ahead,
a puff
of flying light.

Want it! want it!
Wake up at night
crying for it,
walk round all day
needing it.

Till one day
it's there.
Not needed any more
not even wanted.

Look at it without a smile.
Turn away.

NEVER

Should never have done it, never.
Should never have left that country
where I was queen entirely.
Treacherous thaws betrayed me.

That land of I-will-never
gleaming with snow and silence
suited me with its iceblink,
its blue eyes fixed as mirrors.

Set on my peak, I queened it.
It was the spring that took me,
drowning in warmer waters
out to the lands of sometimes.

JUDITH WRIGHT

Here in the lands of sometimes
I stretched out hands lamenting,
but I'm a queen no longer,
melted my snows and glaciers.

They were so strong, so solid,
crystal as tears long frozen.
Here I'm at risk, half-drowning,
wanting my season, winter.

It will return and find me
caught in a depth of water,
freezing unseen in ice-depths,
never again to queen it,

to sit on my peak unmoving
the sceptre cold in my fingers,
my eyes on the blue-eyed glacier.
Should never have left it, never.

FOREVER

Ah, but I had to leave it.
No one can live there always,
the frost-bound queen of Never.
Once the blood moves, the flood moves,

the thaw begins, the ice-peaks
crumble, dissolve to river,
in which I swim or founder
through the warm lands of sometimes;

swim, drown, but now am human.
Change is my true condition,
to take and give and promise,
to fight and fail and alter.

[I aim towards . . .

JUDITH WRIGHT

I aim towards Forever,
but that is no one's country,
till in perhaps one moment,
dying, I'll recognise it;

those peaks not ice but sunlit
from sources past my knowing,
its beauty of completion
the end of being human.

HAROLD STEWART

A Flight of Wild Geese

*Wu Tao-tzŭ, the greatest of Chinese artists, was once commissioned by
the Emperor Ming Huang of the T'ang Dynasty to paint a landscape-roll.
Wu so entered into the spirit of the scene, that he could walk about in
the picture at will. One day he wandered over a distant mountain, and
was never seen again.*

Now Wu Tao-tzŭ, continuing his stroll
Into the landscape on the silken roll,
Comes to the misty shores around a sheet
Of broad water, reaching from his feet
To where a promontory's rocky bar
Lies in the evening sky, it is so far.
Their taper necks stretched out in line of flight,
The wild geese row over at a height;
And while they clang their long-throated cry,
Tow the full moon into an autumn sky.
Diagonals that widen from a wake
Lattice the tranquil surface of the lake
When in the lapping ebb they intervene,
And shake the level creases of its sheen:

A clear grey-green, and yet with depth opaque;
As though four ladies rolling silk should take
Layer on layer of green silk, and of grey,
And stretch them taut across a vacant bay.

To skirt these shores, the painter has to pass
Where the long legs of flowering river-grass
Stand in the margin shallows: feathery rushes
Drawn by his most meticulous of brushes,
Their tufted tops with seed are light and loose
As the soft underdown of a grey goose.
In a flat inlet hereabouts, he sees
How, warily protruding out of these,
A narrow black prow nuzzles the bank:
The grasses thriving here are lush and lank.
Lulled by the idle suction of the tide,
And the slap of lapsing water against the side,
The wily poet snoozing in the stern
With chin on elbow, smiles in unconcern
As round his line a school of mullet feeds.
Under an overcoat of plaited reeds,
He wears the faded purple robe he wore;
To shade his head, a limpet made of straw.
His scant beard and moustaches' straggling hair
Are lightly lifted; flow along the air
Like water-weed that sways this way and that;
And the two fish-tailed ribbons from his hat
Follow them, flapping with a fugal motion.

To bait this odd angler is the notion
The artist forms, for judging by his creel,
Necessity will be his evening meal.

Wu Tao-tzŭ:

'Among the Hundred Surnames, mine is Wu.
Pardon my mannerless presumption, who,
Ancient and solitary one, are you?'

[That rustic archly . . .

That rustic archly opens up one eye
To view this doze-disturbing stranger by;
Yawns like a fox, and stretches to arouse
His cramped limbs from their pictorial drowse.

The Old Fisherman:

'I came here twenty years ago or more,
And yet these hands have never once before
Shaken themselves in salutation's hold.
Then I was Chang Chih-ho. But now the Old
Fisherman of the Waters and the Mists
Conveys of what my way of life consists.'

Wu Tao-tzŭ:

'Why did you quit humanity and home
And choose this wilderness in which to roam?
Why in a humble sampan hold aloof,
Its wicker cradle as your only roof?'

Chang Chih-ho:

'I find it serves quite well to keep me dry.
After the autumn rains stop, and the sky
Clears rapidly, all space shall cover me.
The moonrise, pale and golden, on the sea
Fulfils my modest wishes for a door;
And the sea's jade pavement lays the floor.
These, with the valley walls, make up my home.
What do you mean by saying that I roam?
Here cares and creditors no more infest
The house of mind. Its poverty is rest.
Possessing nothing, I am not possessed.
The State's a monstrous and amorphous plan,
Man's mobilized insanity, and man
Believes it real. Afraid of being free,
He fights to keep the cangue, and cannot flee.
An intimate I would far rather be
Of the white gull which climbs and squalls aloud
Sailing across that black cliff of cloud,
Than have the freedom of my spirit furled
And flung upon the dust-heap of the world.'

Wu Tao-tzŭ:

'From vanity of rank you may retire;
The lust to rule, that menial desire,
The web of power, possessions which degrade—
These you may shun: you cannot thus evade
Your unlived life, the fate you left unpaid.'

Chang Chih-ho:

'No debts or duties did I set aside;
And one who under Su Tsung occupied
The post of minister, was no misfit:
I fled not from the world, but into it.
What other, pray, could I escape to? I'm
Still in this world. I've been here all the time.'

Wu Tao-tzŭ:

'Go where you will, you take your troubled mind,
Whose fears you cannot face, nor leave behind.
In vain your doubts and sorrows you suppress;
In vain avoid society's distress:
Escape has no road from its loneliness.'

Chang Chih-ho:

'An Emperor's entreaty I would spurn;
I have no inclination to return
To where the simple way is smothered in
The court's incessant fuss; where dust and din
Cover the capital, as with a pall;
Where I could have no peace of mind at all.
The case of Chuang Tzŭ doubtless you recall?
Two high officials from the State of Ch'u,
Who called upon him for an interview,
While he was fishing in the river P'u,
Announced, "Our Prince proposes to transfer
The government to you—an office, sir,
Only your wisdom can administer."
The Taoist did not deign to turn his head.

[With rod in hand, . . .

With rod in hand, he watched his line and said,
"In Ch'u there is a tortoise which they hold
Sacred for divination, so I'm told.
It has been dead three thousand years, and since
Kept in a covered casket by the Prince,
Who heats its shell in his ancestral shrine
And reads the cracks in order to divine.
Given the choice when caught, which would it choose?
To stay alive, draggling its tail in ooze;
Or to be reverenced by men, but dead?"
"To be alive, of course," the officials said.
"Off with you then, and let me," he replied,
"Waggle my tail, too, in the muddy tide."
And some declare the sage washed out his ears
To cleanse them of political ideas;
And that downstream a cowherd then complained
The waters were polluted and profaned.'

Wu Tao-tzŭ:

'But see! The skeins of geese arriving span
The sky and write the words for "one" and "man".'

Chang Chih-ho:

'And yet they have been here since time began.'

Down the sky in file the wild geese tack,
Slanting their obliquely angled track
Toward the estuary's bank of sand
With blocks of basalt strewn along the strand.
The leader there comes skidding in, to sit
On a long splash, for the sheer sport of it:
His tail-feathers fan to brake the flight;
And webbed feet and red legs alight,
As if fixed in a clear aquamarine,
So still the surface-water is, and green.
There he stands upright in the water-rings,
Throws out his breast, and flaps his wide wings;
There ducks, to ladle over back and head
Wingfuls of water; shakes his tail to shed
Superfluous drops; and washing over, grooms
Down smooth and trim his toilet-ruffled plumes;

And then into a comfortable unrest
Worries the pin-plumage of his breast.
More glide in after him. The others land
Pinions aloft, and settle on the sand,
Where flat snapping bills hiss and contest
Scraps of aquatic weed that one possessed.
Pushing a fold of glass against the stream,
One paddles in pursuit of his own gleam.
Another stoops his pliant neck to sip
This running ripple with the glassy lip,
And elevates it after every dip.
A third, whose bill tugged at the wavering weeds,
Lifts their dripping ribbons up, and feeds.
Riding its undulating ebb, the fleet
Of geese sets sail upon the glaucous sheet;
But a snapped stick startles one among
Them. Instantly the floating flock is sprung.
Low over the water skims each pair:
The downbeat of the wing-tip in the air
Touching the upbeat of its image there.
Once in the central air, they travel south
Beyond the sandspit at the river's mouth,
Beyond the dim horizon. All are gone.
But, like a flock of feathers dropped upon
The refluent air after their motion's flown,
A soft flocculence of cloud is strown;
And hovers, as invisible waves of wake
Diverge, and on the mountains sprayless break.

Wu Tao-tzŭ:

'They have migrated to a warmer clime.'

Chang Chih-ho:

'They will be here now till the end of time.'

A light breeze that springs up off the bay,
Bending the plumed grasses all one way
And carrying their seeded fluff astray,

               [Just as suddenly drops.

Just as suddenly drops. At once the rushes'
Thicket of dry whispers thins and hushes
To a faint rustle. Nothing stirs the brake.
Chang winds his fishing-line in from the lake.

Wu's face is lost in an astonished look,
For from it dangles neither bait nor hook!

Wu Tao-tzŭ:

'How ever do you hope to catch a stray
Tadpole, though you angle here all day?
This is no way to get a bite. You need
An iron hook, a juicy worm or weed
For bait, with float and sinker, if you wish
To offer some enticement to a fish.'

Hinting that he knows more than one would think,
The artful Taoist slyly tips a wink:

Chang Chih-ho:

'Ah! But that's not what I was fishing for!'

He poles his lean punt away from shore.
The layered strands of vapour closing in,
Leave no trace that he has even been . . .

Into infinite distance, sad and clear,
Recede the miles of autumn atmosphere:
With pale citrine tone, the watery light
That shines out after rain, washes their height.
The autumn mountain, swept as neat and clean
As the tidy winds can, reclines serene:
No twig is out of place; no leaf is seen
Of all that tarnished ruin of gold which lay
Underfoot so densely, yesterday.
The earth has claimed their tribute to decay.
Upon its sides the naked forests brood,
Locked in a crystalline disquietude;
And looped with sleeping vines and beards of moss,
Despair for want of leaves, the season's loss.

Each tall, gaunt, calligraphic tree
Forked against the light's sour clarity,
Soars with static branches, sparse and bare,
In the remote and disappointed air.
An empty vast, the autumn waters lie
Merging into the open sea of sky.
Slowly the ebb goes out, and from the height
Drains away the westering tide of light.

Ah! The evening's mood is growing late.
The peasant enters now his brushwood gate.
The garden overgrown with grass and weed,
Where spires of wild lettuce run to seed,
Lies drenched with recent rain, and desolate.
A sulphur-coloured butterfly chases its mate
Over the fence with devious flutterings:
They are the only autumn leaves with wings.
The altered air that chills the end of day
Makes the fishing-nets and tackle sway
Gently over on their bamboo poles.
And now a village bell remotely tolls
The still and solemn hour; now holds its peace.
The work of men, the year's affairs decrease.
Now lamps are lit in windows far and near.
See! Through the yellow dusk their flames appear.
Within the peasant's hut two suppers wait.

Ah! The evening's mood is growing late.

A smooth moon in the laminated fog
That weaves the stagnant levels of a bog
With trails of gossamer, is hanging low
Its pallid disc, too early yet to glow.
Beside this languid marsh the artist walks.
Still to the withered old lotus stalks
The rattling seeds in conic pods adhere;
The flounced leaves float, tattered and sere;
And sere the willow leaves spin as they sift
On a despondent pond their falling drift.

[There like sallow . . .

There like sallow sampans they are thrust
Aimlessly along by a tired gust
Into a backwater. There some dust
Is spent, and settles, and the waste becalms
Among an undergrowth of roots with arms
For now the world of nature is subdued
And grave with an autumnal lassitude.

Out on the lake a solitary sail
Goes home into the world. With this detail
The subtle Taoist in his fishing-smack
Sketches in the landscape's only lack.
Its blind of white grows smaller, outward blown.
One last goose wings on its way alone:
A hook of ink against the silken sky,
Gone with the echo of a far high cry...

        Wu Tao-tzŭ:

'A lone goose and a lone sail depart:
They do not leave the shore, they leave the heart.'

               —1944.

JAMES McAULEY

Envoi for a Book of Poems

There the blue-green gums are a fringe of remote disorder
And the brown sheep poke at my dreams along the hillsides;
And there in the soil, in the season, in the shifting airs,
Comes the faint sterility that disheartens and derides.

JAMES McAULEY

Where once was a sea is now a salty sunken desert,
A futile heart within a fair periphery;
The people are hard-eyed, kindly, with nothing inside them,
The men are independent but you could not call them free.

And I am fitted to that land as the soul is to the body,
I know its contractions, waste, and sprawling indolence;
They are in me and its triumphs are my own,
Hard-won in the thin and bitter years without pretence.

Beauty is order and good chance in the artesian heart
And does not wholly fail, though we impede;
Though the reluctant and uneasy land resent
The gush of waters, the lean plough, the fretful seed.

The Incarnation of Sirius

In that age, the great anagram of God
Had bayed the planets from the rounds they trod,
And gathered the fixed stars in a shining nation
Like restless birds that flock before migration.

For the millennial instinct of new flight
Resolved the antimony that fixed their light;
And echoing in the troubled soul of Earth,
Quickened a virgin's womb, to bring to birth

What scarce was human: a rude avatar
That glistened with the enclosed wrath of a star
The woman died in pangs, before she had kissed
The monstrous form of God's antagonist.

But at its showing forth, the poets cried
In a strange tongue; hot mouths prophesied
The coolness of the bloody vintage-drops:
'Let us be drunk at least, when the world stops!'

[Anubis-headed, . . .

JAMES McAULEY

Anubis-headed, the heresiarch
Sprang to a height, fire-sinewed in the dark,
And his ten fingers, bracketed on high,
Were a blazing candelabrum in the sky.

The desert lion antiphonally roared;
The tiger's sinews quivered like a chord;
Man smelt the blood beneath his brother's skin
And in a loving hate the sword went in.

And then the vision sank, bloody and aborted.
The stars that with rebellion had consorted
Fled back in silence to their former stations.
Over the giant face of dreaming nations

The centuries-thick coverlet was drawn.
Upon the huddled breast Aldebaran
Still glittered with its sad alternate fire:
Blue as of memory, red as of desire.

Invocation

Radiant Muse, my childhood's nurse,
Who gave my wondering mouth to taste
The fragrant honeycomb of verse;
And later smilingly embraced
My boyhood, ripening its crude
Harsh vigour in your solitude:

Compose the mingling thoughts that crowd
Upon me to a lucid line;
Teach me at last to speak aloud
In words that are no longer mine;
For at your touch, discreet, profound,
Ten thousand years softly resound.

I do not now revolt, or quarrel
With the paths you make me tread,
But choose the honeycomb and laurel
And walk with patience towards the dead;
Expecting, where my rest is stayed,
A welcome in that windless shade.

Because

My father and my mother never quarrelled.
They were united in a kind of love
As daily as the *Sydney Morning Herald*,
Rather than like the eagle or the dove.

I never saw them casually touch,
Or show a moment's joy in one another.
Why should this matter to me now so much?
I think it bore more hardly on my mother,

Who had more generous feeling to express.
My father had dammed up his Irish blood
Against all drinking praying fecklessness,
And stiffened into stone and creaking wood.

His lips would make a switching sound, as though
Spontaneous impulse must be kept at bay.
That it was mainly weakness I see now,
But then my feelings curled back in dismay.

Small things can pit the memory like a cyst:
Having seen other fathers greet their sons,
I put my childish face up to be kissed
After an absence. The rebuff still stuns

My blood. The poor man's curt embarrassment
At such a delicate proffer of affection
Cut like a saw. But home the lesson went:
My tenderness thenceforth escaped detection.

[My mother sang . . .

My mother sang *Because*, and *Annie Laurie*,
White Wings, and other songs; her voice was sweet.
I never gave enough, and I am sorry;
But we were all closed in the same defeat.

People do what they can; they were good people,
They cared for us and loved us. Once they stood
Tall in my childhood as the school, the steeple.
How can I judge without ingratitude?

Judgment is simply trying to reject
A part of what we are because it hurts.
The living cannot call the dead collect:
They won't accept the charge, and it reverts.

It's my own judgment day that I draw near,
Descending in the past, without a clue,
Down to that central deadness: the despair
Older than any hope I ever knew.

ROSEMARY DOBSON

The Bystander

I am the one who looks the other way,
In any painting you may see me stand
Rapt at the sky, a bird, an angel's wing,
While others kneel, present the myrrh, receive
The benediction from the radiant hand.

I hold the horses while the knights dismount
And draw their swords to fight the battle out;
Or else in dim perspective you may see
My distant figure on the mountain road
When in the plains the hosts are put to rout.

I am the silly soul who looks too late,
The dullard dreaming, second from the right.
I hang upon the crowd, but do not mark
(Cap over eyes) the slaughtered Innocents,
Or Icarus, his downward-plunging flight.

Once in a Garden—back view only there—
How well the painter placed me, stroke on stoke,
Yet scarcely seen among the flowers and grass—
I heard a voice say, 'Eat,' and would have turned—
I often wonder who it was that spoke.

Country Press

Under the dusty print of hobnailed boot,
Strewn on the floor the papers still assert
In ornamental gothic, swash italics
And bands of printer's flowers (traditional)
Mixed in a riot of typographic fancy,
This is the *Western Star*, the Farmer's Guide,
The Voice of Progress for the Nyngle District.
Page-proofs of double-spread with running headlines
Paper the walls, and sets of cigarette-cards
Where pouter-bosomed showgirls still display
The charms that dazzled in the nineteen hundreds.
Through gaping slats
Latticed with sun the ivy tendrils fall
Twining the disused platen thrust away
Under a pall of dust in nineteen-twenty.
Draw up a chair, sit down. Just shift the galleys.
You say you have a notice? There's no one dies
But what we know about it. Births, deaths and marriages,
Council reports, wool prices, river-heights,
The itinerant poem and the classified ads—
They all come homewards to the *Western Star*.

[Joe's our typesetter. Meet . . .

Joe's our type-setter. Meet Joe Burrell. Joe's
A promising lad—and Joe, near forty-seven,
Peers from a tennis-shade and, smiling vaguely,
Completes the headline for the Baptist Social.
The dance, the smoke-oh, and the children's picnic
Down by the river-flats beneath the willows—
They all come homewards and Joe sets them all,
Between the morning and the mid-day schooner.
Oh, *Western Star* that bringest all to fold,
The yarding sales, the champion shorthorn bull,
And Williams' pain-relieving liniment,
When I shall die
Set me up close against my fellow-men,
Cheer that cold column headed 'Deaths' with flowers,
Or mix me up with Births and Marriages;
Surround the tragic statement of my death
With euchre-drives and good-times-had-by-all
That, with these warm concomitants of life
Jostled and cheered, in lower-case italics
I shall go homewards in the *Western Star.*

GWEN HARWOOD

'I am the Captain of My Soul'

The human body is the best picture of the human soul.
LUDWIG WITTGENSTEIN

But the Captain is drunk, and the crew
hauling hard on his windlass of fury are whipped
by his know-nothing rage. Their terror
troubles the sunlight. 'Now tell me,'

the Captain says, as his drunkenness
drifts into tears, 'what's to keep me
at ease in this harbour?'
                              'We'll tell you,'
say Hands, 'in our headlong chase through a fugue

for three voices, you heard a fourth voice naming
divisions of silence. We'll summon
that voice once again, it may tell you
of marvels wrung from sorrow endured.'
'We have seen,' say Eyes, 'how in Venice
the steps of churches open and close
like marble fans under water.'

'You can rot in your sockets,' the Captain cries.

'I have children,' says Body, haloed
in tenderness, firm in ripeness still.
'I grew gross with their stress, I went spinning
in a vortex of pain. I gave my breast
and its beauty to nourish their heedless growth.
They jump on my shadow in mischievous joy.
On their lives your astonishing sorrows
flow easy as water on marble steps.'

'Lass sie betteln gehn!' roars the Captain
as his old wounds burn, and he gulps
from his flagon of grief. 'You servants, you things,
stand up there! *You* with the ageing choir-boy face,
and *you* with your facile dexterity, *you*
with your marble hallucinations, COME!'

Hands, eyes, body keel to the void as the drunken
Captain sings in his wilderness of water.

GWEN HARWOOD

In Brisbane

By the old bridge in flaring sunlight
a ghost is waiting, with my face
of twenty years ago, to show me
the paths I never can retrace.

Here as of old upon the river
float light's beguiling images.
Over a quilt of blue the branches
bend with domestic tenderness.

Here, to my blood's exalted rhythm,
silly with love I'd pace for hours
sifting the piecemeal revelations
of life and time through falling flowers.

Intemperate ghost, who longed to hazard
the pure space of experience,
to bid unheard-of constellations
form from their joyful elements:

these trees that cannot hold their blossom,
the public handsomeness of stone
remain. Your grand abstractions shimmered
like light on water, and are gone.

My ghost, my self, most intimate stranger
standing beneath these lyric trees
with your one wineglassful of morning
snatched from the rushing galaxies,

bright-haired and satin-lipped you offer
the youth I shall not taste again.
I know, I bear to know, your future
unlooked-for love, undreamed-of pain.

With your untempered spirit shatter
the glass of time that keeps apart
what was and is.
                Through fractured sunlight
I see a less-than-shadow pass

to light again. A cloud of blossom
drifts on the water's changing face
from the blue trees unfolding summer
above my head in sunlit space.

All Souls'

Circumflex firs. At last the sun
buried all day, appears and fills
the snow with green. Too late, it is
already evening, and the hills

sharpen the silence of cold skies.
One ray, with a grandmother's finger,
tender and dry, strokes on the glass.
Below the firs deep shadows linger,

while clouds exchange evasive tones.
Brittle, frail as an insect wing,
last light vibrates, is trapped within
night's web, is gone, and wandering

inhuman-human presences
swarm to my lighted candle's flame,
in metaphors of silence beg
a human syllable, a name.

GWEN HARWOOD

Person to Person

So we meet as of old where the rosevine
is tied to a trellis with rags, and the flowers
push us left to that place we know; now the town
with its murmuring ceaseless invention
of old, friendly ghosts among tree-clustered greens
lies quiet below.

I speak of those years when I lived
walled alive in myself, left with nothing
but the inward search for joy, for a word
that would ruffle the plumage of mind to reach
its tenderest down; when consuming
myself I endured, but could not change.

Through the rents in a wall the fresh weeds
are labouring for sunlight.
                          This perfect joy
excludes any feeling of joy, and we laugh
at the world and its crazy perspectives,
at the suburbs' impotent trimmings
and guilt-driven labour,

and talk, with a deeper passion
than delight in our skill.
                        I reach to take
your hand, and a thorn from the rosevine
rakes blood from my wrist.
                        I cannot hear
what you say as a child comes to wake me
by scraping his nails on my arm.

Who grows old in a dream, who can taste
the ripe wholeness of absence? And who can summon
by light the incredible likeness of sleep?
From this fading dream as useless now
as a torn-off wing I wake to embrace
the stubborn presence of life.

KATH WALKER

We are going

for Grannie Coolwell

They came in to the little town
A semi-naked band subdued and silent,
All that remained of their tribe.
They came here to the place of their old bora ground
Where now the many white men hurry about like ants.
Notice of estate agent reads: 'Rubbish May Be Tipped Here.'
Now it half covers the traces of the old bora ring.
They sit and are confused, they cannot say their thoughts:
'We are as strangers here now, but the white tribe are the
    strangers.
We belong here, we are of the old ways.
We are the corroboree and the bora ground,
We are the old sacred ceremonies, the laws of the elders.
We are the wonder tales of Dream Time, the tribal legends
    told.
We are the past, the hunts and the laughing games, the
    wandering camp fires.
We are the lightning-bolt over Gaphembah Hill
Quick and terrible,
And the Thunderer after him, that loud fellow.
We are the quiet daybreak paling the dark lagoon.
We are the shadow-ghosts creeping back as the camp fires
    burn low.
We are nature and the past, all the old ways
Gone now and scattered.
The scrubs are gone, the hunting and the laughter.
The eagle is gone, the emu and the kangaroo are gone from
    this place.
The bora ring is gone.
The corroboree is gone.
And we are going.'

Ixion

Turning and re-turning,
   the wheel returns once more,
once more the circus-master
   beckons through the door.
Will nothing stop the shadows'
   convolutions on the floor?

Will nothing stop the shadows?
   Must I once again perform
the usual limited number
   of variations from the norm?
Though the sky seems set for thunder
   there is never any storm.

Though the sky seems set for thunder,
   rest assured it will not rain;
at least till the appropriate season
   has everything in train.
There is never any reversal
   for the slayer and the slain.

There is never any reversal,
   the axe achieves the block,
denial produces only
   the crowing of the cock.
Turning and re-turning;
   no one stops the clock.

Apocalypse in Springtime

So I was in the city on this day:
and suddenly a darkness
came upon the city like night,
and it was night;
and all around me, and on either hand,

both above and below me,
there was—so it seemed—a dissolving
and a passing away.

And I listened with my ears, and heard
a great rushing
as the winds of the world left the earth,
and then there was silence,
and no sound, neither the roar of the city,
nor the voices of people,
nor the singing of birds, nor the crying
of any animal;
for the world that was audible had vanished
and passed away.

And I stretched forth both my hands,
but could touch nothing,
neither the buildings, nor the passers-by,
neither could I feel
the pavement underneath my feet,
nor the parts of my body;
for the world that was tangible had vanished
and passed away.

And I looked around and about me,
and could see nothing,
neither the heavens, nor the sea, nor the earth,
nor the waters under it;
for the world that was visible had vanished
and passed away.

In my nostrils there was a fleeting
fume of corruption,
and on my tongue a dying taste
of putrefaction,
and then these departed, and there was nothing;
for the world that was scent,
and the world that was savour had vanished
and passed away.

[And all around me, and . . .

And all around me, and on either hand,
both above and below me,
there was nothing, and before me and behind;
for all of the fivefold
worlds of the world had vanished
and passed away.

And all my possessions of pride
had been taken from me,
and the wealth of my esteem stricken,
and the crown of my kingdom,
and all my human glory,
and I had nothing, and I was nothing;
for all things sensible had vanished
and passed away.

And I was alone in nothing,
and stood at the bar
of nothing, was accused by nothing,
and defended by nothing,
and nothing deliberated judgment
against me.

And the arbitrament of the judgment
was revealed to me.

Then the nothing faded into nothing,
and that into nothing,

and I was alone in a darkness like night,
but it was not night;
then the darkness faded into darkness,
and that into darkness,
and there was no light—but only
emptiness,
and a voice in the void lamenting
and dying away.

MAX HARRIS

The Tantanoola Tiger

There in the bracken was the ominous spoor mark,
Huge, splayed, deadly, and quiet as breath,
And all around lay bloodied and dying,
Staring dumbly into their several eternities,
The rams that Mr Morphett loved as sons.

Not only Tantanoola, but at Mount Schanck
The claw welts patterned the saplings
With mysteries terrible as Egypt's demons,
More evil than the blueness of the Lakes,
And less than a mile from the homestead, too.

Sheep died more rapidly than the years
Which the tiger ruled in tooth and talk,
And it padded from Beachport to the Border,
While blood streamed down the minds of the folk
Of Mount Gambier, Tantanoola, of Casterton.

Oh this tiger was seen all right, grinning,
Yellow and gleaming with satin stripes:
Its body arched and undulated through the tea-tree;
In this land of dead volcanoes it was a flame,
It was a brightness, it was the glory of death,

It was fine, this tiger, a sweet shudder
In the heath and everlastings of the Border,
A roc bird up the ghostly ring-barked gums
Of Mingbool Swamp, a roaring fate
Descending on the mindless backs of grazing things.

Childhoods burned with its burning eyes,
Tantanoola was a magic playground word,
It rushed through young dreams like a river
And it had lovers in Mr Morphett and Mr Marks
For the ten long hunting unbelieving years.

[Troopers and blacks . . .

121

Troopers and blacks made safari, Africa-fashion,
Pastoral Quixotes swayed on their ambling mounts,
Lost in invisible trails. The red-faced
Young Lindsay Gordons of the Mount
Tormented their heartbeats in the rustling nights

While the tiger grew bigger and clear as an axe.
'A circus once abandoned a tiger cub.'
This was the creed of the hunters and poets.
'A dingo that's got itself too far south'
The grey old cynics thundered in their beers,

And blows were swapped and friendships broken,
Beauty burst on a loveless and dreary people,
And their moneyed minds broke into singing
A myth; these soured and tasteless settlers
Were Greeks and Trojans, billabong troubadours,

Plucking their themes at the picnic races
Around the kegs in the flapping canvas booths.
On the waist-coats sharks' teeth swung in time,
And old eyes, sharply seamed and squinting,
Opened mysteriously in misty musical surprise,

Until the day Jack Heffernan made camp
By a mob of sheep on the far slope of Mt Schanck
And woke to find the tiger on its haunches,
Bigger than a mountain, love, or imagination,
Grinning lazily down on a dying ewe,

And he drew a bead and shot it through the head.
Look down, oh mourners of history, poets,
Look down on the black and breeding volcanic soil,
Lean on your fork in this potato country,
Regard the yellowed fangs and quivering claws

Of a mangy and dying Siberian wolf.
It came as a fable or a natural image
To pace the bars of these sunless minds,
A small and unimpressive common wolf
In desperately poor and cold condition.

It howled to the wattle when it swam ashore
From the wreck of the foundered Helena,
Smelt death and black snakes and tight lips
On every fence-post and slip-rail.
It was three foot six from head to tail.

Centuries will die like swatted blowflies
Before word or wolf will work a tremor
Of tenderness in the crusty knuckles
Around the glasses in the Tantanoola pub
Where its red bead eyes now stare towards the sun.

On throwing a copy of the New Statesman into the Coorong

Through the car window goes Kingsley Martin.
With his neat typography and ageing Fabian gentility!
It is good to Whitmanise now and again.
It flushes the liver where the soul sits like an owl.

Kingsley flaps and tatters on a branch of wild tobacco.

The clay and water meet a hundred yards away
In a shivering froth. Like tumbleweed it breaks
And rolls with the wind into the dunes of saltbush.
The great Snake Slut has sudded the water's edge
For forty miles, and washed her tribe of their scaly skins.

Come December, Kingsley, there'll be pround conclaves
Of gleaming bellies and diamond backs. You'll love it.

If this dead land traps another rise of sea
And the tide laps the Ki-Ki signpost (Lonely Track.
No Water. RAA) the lizards will top
The fence posts. One frilled head to one signpost
For sinewed miles that never end . . . a dream
Of St Stylites, great horny frills, licking tongues,
And death.

[The ageless Slut . . .

The ageless Slut trains her spawn
To dance. Pavanne. Pavanne. Ten thousand
Black snakes gather at a time, stand up
In the water and rock like lilies on their stems
In the wind, in the winter solstice, in time.

You'll not be lonely. See that tea-tree,
(Uprooted, its struggling stilled as the bogged carcase
Of a steer half under clay) with the greatcoat
Of Nineteen Fourteen tied at the gap in its roots,
It is the front door to half-caste Charlie's home.
Knock. Knock. Battling with his plonk,
He and his tree are one, man and castle,
Being and reason. Love them together, man!

The wind is no longer serrating sideways down the sand.
It is the hour of the Bloody Great Drongo,
The hour of the sand fox, for the brumby to edge uneasily
With sway back and collapsed belly to the pastures
Of saltbush. The fretful clan of Murray magpies
Swoop clear of the sparrowhawk, leave him to peck
And claw the prey to the slowest promethean death.

The pallid sun sinks, one might think, into the bar
Of the Meningie pub. Far away. Sleep well Kingsley.

DOROTHY HEWETT

In Moncur Street

It's twenty years ago and more
since first I came to Moncur Street,
and live with Aime and Alf among
the boarders on the second floor.

DOROTHY HEWETT

The stew was burnt, the budgie sang,
as Aime walked home the church-bells rang,
she banged the pots, ring-ding-a-ding,
she'd lost at Housie in the Spring.

But Sammy Smiles (that lovely man),
still visits her on Saturday,
Beat runs a book, and little Fay
whines in the stairwell every day
                    in Moncur Street
                    in Moncur Street.

Alf rose before the morning light,
and took a chopper in his hand;
he chopped and chopped in Oxford Street,
'Alf runs around without his head,
he's like a chook,' said Aime
                and sighed
for Sammy Smiles (that lovely man),

and Sunny Corner where she played
at 'Ladies' in the willow's shade.
At sunset by the empty shops
they swapped their dusty acid drops:
who lounges in the crystal air,
but Sammy Smiles, with marcelled hair!

I woke up in the darkest night,
knew all the world had caught alight.
The surf was pounding in the weather,
and Moncur Street was mine forever.
The little bat upon the stair
came out and flapped: it wasn't there,

the snapshot album turned and turned,
the stew caught fire, the budgie burned,
the pensioners at drafts and dreams,
picked bugs between their trouser seams.

                    [And Sammy Smiles . . .

And Sammy Smiles (that lovely man!)
and Aime and Alf and little Fay,
and Beat and Bert and betting slips,
the man I loved, the child I bore,
have all gone under Bondi's hills,
and will return here nevermore,
     in Moncur Street
     in Moncur Street.

Alf starts up his steady snore,
'Them Bondi sandhills paved with gold,
I could've bought them for a song.'
The home brew bursts behind the door.
Aime lies upon her back and sighs:
'In Sunny Corner by the store
Sam kissed me once when I turned four.'

Dreams are deep and love is long:
she turns upon her other side.

Miss Hewett's Shenanigans

They call, 'The Prince has come,'
& I swan down in astrakan & fur,
the lemon curtains blown against the light,
the scent of lilac on the balconies.
In the entrance hall
the Prince is standing
    staring at my thighs.
He mounts, how cold the marble
underneath my buttocks.
As he rides he calls me
    'whore' & 'princess'.
A platinum crooner, old as Alice Faye,
belts out bad ragtime in the empty ballroom.
The Prince, buttoning his fly,
is doing push-ups & demanding saunas.
Two giant Ghanaians smile & kiss my hand.

DOROTHY HEWETT

Snow piles like roses
                up against the panes,
the waiter brings 'Ogonyok',
SINYAVSKY'S FLED & SOLZHENITSYN'S EXILED.
The lights all fail,
the electrician's pinching bulbs
from the chandeliers, shoving them
                down his shirtfront.
Outside in the dark at Lenin's tomb
they endlessly queue for weeping
                at the waxworks.
The Prince is in the Conference Hall,
listening through headphones
to a speech in seven languages.
Handsome Yugoslav colonels
discreetly try my doorknobs.
Exhausted, we sleep among carved bears
with ashtrays in their paws,
he refuses, once again, to consummate
                our marriage.

Next day we catch the Trans-Siberian
to Peking; from the observation car
we watch two wolves pacing out the train,
the Prince throws pennies to Manchurian children.
On the Great Wall he lets the wind blow
through my hair, in the Forbidden City
we listen to the clockwork nightingale.

By Aeroflot we fly in to Berlin,
the Prince will not declare his Camels
                at Checkpoint Charlie,
(An international incident is narrowly averted.)
In the country house of Hitler's wormy mistress
we row on a lake circled with tuber roses.
The Prince, a playboy in a boater hat,
is picking the plastic flowers
                off Heine's statue;

                        [denouncing Nazis he pisses . . .

denouncing Nazis he pisses in the Weimar fountain,
rides with a chignoned spy
                              down Karl Marx Allee.
Tiring of this,
            we climb across The Wall,
the Vopos bow, goosestep & fire a round,
the bullets spurt,
we show our elegant heels.
In West Berlin the Prince
calls for his breakfast, on TV
Brezhnev has cancer, enters the Mayo clinic.

The Prince leafs through his autographs,
Picasso, Gandhi, Garbo, Pasternak,
calls Nabokov long distance, mounts me,
yawns, the Brandenburg Gate whirls
& explodes in the pale Autumn air.
Next morning he leaves,
                  taking all my roubles.

Suffering from migraine
I enter a Retreat
among the Alps I write him
endless letters.
The corridors are full of parasites,
consumptives haemorrhage in their sleety
                                    deckchairs,
in the white nights I masturbate
                        my pillows.

        An aerogramme arrives,
        'The Prince is dead!'
I take up seances,
each night we couple,
circling the empty ballroom
                  to 'Moscow Nights'.
Cockroaches rustle, my thrombosed knee
reeks of its vodka bandage,
the dust settles from the chandelier
                  on his bald head . . .

VINCENT BUCKLEY

Secret Policeman

Pledge me: I had the hangman for a father
And for my mother the immortal State;
My playground was the yard beside the lime-pit,
My play-songs the after-cries of hate.

Admire me: I fill these shining boots,
I am soul expanded to a uniform;
A hired world glitters at my senses,
The smell of blood keeps my blood-stream warm.

Pity me: from a world ruddy with flame
I am tugged in dreams to the first cave again,
And in that humid soil and atmosphere
Lie down each night beside the murdered men.

The dead eyes point the way I go,
The dead hands presage me in air.
I run on shifting pavements, by fired walls
Falling, and weighted lamp-posts everywhere.

from *Golden Builders*

I

The hammers of iron glow down Faraday.
Lygon and Drummond shift under their resonance.
Saws and hammers drawn across the bending air
shuttling like a bow; the saw trembles
the hammers are molten, they flow with quick light
striking; the flush spreads and deepens on the stone.
The drills call the streets together
stretching hall to lecture-room to hospital.

[But prop old walls . . .

But prop old walls with battens of old wood.

Saturday work. Sabbath work. *On this day*
we laid this stone
to open this Sabbath School. Feed My Lambs.

The sun dies half-glowing in the floating brickdust.
suspended between red and saffron.
The colours resonate like a noise; the muscles of mouth
neck shoulders loins arm themselves against it.
Pavements clink like steel; the air soft,
palpable as cork, lets the stone cornices
gasp into it. Pelham surrenders, Grattan
runs leading forward, seeking the garden's breadth, the fearful
edge of green on which the sexes lay.

We have built this Sabbath School. Feed My Lambs.

Evening wanders through my hands and feet
my mouth is cool as the air that now thins
twitching the lights on down winding paths. Everything
leans on this bright cold. In gaps of lanes, in tingling
shabby squares, I hear the crying of the machines.

O Cardigan, Queensberry, Elgin: names of their lordships.
Cardigan, Elgin, Lygon: Shall I find here my Lord's grave?

II

God knows what it is about Town Halls.
I've lived next door to three of them,
in small crouched brick houses, like an admirer,
beside their shadows, their arguments, their clocks,
the Labor Party rooms, and the Police Station.

Once, night after night, I listened
to the rats flutter in the blank stone furnace,
'the old stove'. The best place to build in.
They grew their family there as if the old stove
were a dry cave on a mountain.
Their nerves were strong as mine.

When I smoked them out and killed them
they backed up like Spartans until, cornered,
tails twitching at the locked door,
they came screaming at my knees.

Now I kill on a small scale.

In the cleared space, under the touching branches,
I shovel in the trash for burning,
papers, foil, cartons. In the shielded sun
the tiny separate flames
jump like candle-light. The smudged bricks
get back their flush of red. And the small
unkillable bodies of the centipedes
rush from wall to wall, the movement
an unvoiced shriek in the loam-like damp,
unsnappable, twisting, shellac bodies.
But I kill them with a spade between the bricks.
And find something like pleasure in it
        (of a sort you'd never dare to tell the
        unforgiving and compassionate young).

III

Practising Not Dying (i)

Even if there'd been prayers
Left for an hour, not quite prayed,
Hanging like chill strings in the air,
You'd have no choice

You'd have to lie back, trying
Vaguely for a normal
Pulse. One knee crooked on the other
As if no more could happen

To you, already stone, with a limewhite
Skin—your mouth
An unslaked taste. Waiting, knowing
Anything can happen.

                    [The rasp of water . . .

The rasp of water running somewhere.
You go to splash it on your face
Coils of browned tap-thick water
Settle over your hands. You don't

Dry them, you lie back again.
Two or three small house-flies
Settle, flaying at your mouth.
Your hand bumps on your cheekbone

As you go to flick them off.

If you lie long enough
Who knows what will settle
On your face or hand: a shredded
Fragment of carbon

Drifted through the window, a globule
Of hot weld,
A dried morsel of cypress,
A seed from the uprooted spiky bush.

IV

They are digging everywhere. From street to street
the sound stitches pavements together. The drill
vibrates with the vibration of his muscles.
He leans it away from his loins
until he can carry himself
on its weight, it moves in, attaches him
to the stone earth that rejects him
and to the tiny insistent grassblade.
It may have rivers under it
or soil traced with salt jungles
or a field of oil
not quite motionless, its unrevealed light
shifting like Elysium.

The watcher would see nothing of this.

Would see nothing
of the next street, either. She comes, five minutes early,
brushing the cold brick of each house
with her fingertips. Fluttered into a head-back
confidence. The child like a bolt in her womb.
Inside the small terrace house, she waits
on linoleum. The abortionist
has the skill of an engineer
his eyes brood like a pilot's. His hand is steady
as he lifts it away from her sweating legs.

So she imagines that something cried
weakly at the furnace door
wrapped in trash paper.

I see nothing of this. I look towards the hospital
through a coma of white, the rows of windows
edged through stone. There, once, I found my children.
Today, in Faraday, behind the school's dull turrets,
I heard the crying of the machines.

V

Purblind walls
peeled back like an onion-skin.

Two miles, twelve months away,
Pieter, when he came back into the room,
stooping, almost running,
swayed against the doorpost,
the scissors hung in his hand. Crying
'Have I killed you, brother.
O Christ, brother, have I killed you?'
Where his eyes were,
hollows of mist.
The dead man was no blood-relation.

We have built these squares, these towers. Feed My Lambs.

[In a million . . .

In a million rooms
the Seven O'Clock Early News:
a hot, level voice
vibrates the thin walls.
Each radio
listens to its neighbour
with hot, level voice.

Round the stone corner, in a dark
warm place, with the sky in sight,
and a tree nearby, its long leaves crouched about it,
she burnt herself to death. Almost too shy
to go and buy the petrol. That night
I was drinking, to the background
of soft halloo-ing Irish music,
arguing Vietnam.

XXVII

As the car stooped, seemed to pause
on the crest of the macadam hill
and the staining grass paddocks led north
to the long blue mountains

                                    three things converging
suddenly   the thought of hot bread
entered me   the car
filled with burning, driftsmell   in the air
miles away, in front of cloudcover,
a great tuft of burnsmudge,
motionless   slowly dissolving

        each car rides on its shadow

Sunday grinds on
Sunday. On our right the brief church
in its paddock, in its fine-tempered stone,
lives under noise. Ropes of noise trail up. The jet-planes
sweat in the air. At every boom
the mortar shakes out in dust
and the trim stones lean together

VINCENT BUCKLEY

earth shaken from the root   or marrow
from the bone.

We are travelling
towards my timber birthplace
and the wilderness of flies (Somehow
damp grass surrounds a house with heat)
and the dogs paused above the creek.

And my Lord's grave? His grave?

J. R. ROWLAND

In Southeast Asia

(VIET NAM)

*Que ne vous ai-je rencontrés, sauvages imprévus qui
présentiez aux navigateurs des fruits en forme de cornes
sur des plateaux barbares, tandis que des coupoles
apparaissaient entre les palmes! O découvertes . . .*
       ANDRÉ MALRAUX: *Tentation de l'Occident*

I

O discoveries!
        the landscape developing
In palm and mangrove and watercoloured plain
Hatched with canals, before the steady ship
That noses up a narrow yellow water
Under a rosy sky.
        Silence
Of the fall of evening.
        Far away

       [A mysterious horizon . . .

A mysterious horizon ledged with cloud
A single pointed mountain out of the plain.

What people build
These sharp-roofed houses thicketed in bamboos,
Whose boats, angular and delicately shaped,
Are painted with eyes at either end; whose smokes
Gesture from distances; whose cranes at wells
Rising and falling, arching slender necks,
Stoop like waterbirds among the ricefields?
Suddenly, at hand, a rivervillage:
Huts, crazy jetties, pyramids of white jars,
And waterbuffaloes glistening fat as slugs

Or carcasses awash blow in the near mudponds.
From their backs the spidernaked children
Watch from averted faces our clean ship
Invade their singular country, half-land half-water.

It is not yet the imagined Orient
This green familiar unfamiliar landscape
Sinister, populous and yet hidden.
Stand; and let your mind pierce the horizon
To the expected city: walls and towers
Temples of finials and trembling bells
Interiors dusky with incense, hung with banners
Bearing unknown inscriptions; many objects
Of bronze and lacquer that glint looming in darkness;
Steps of stone softened by multitudes;
Ancient images, elaborate usages
And all the apparatus of the East.

So might one come, up the stalesmelling river
To the wharves where all day and night the coolies
Chant unloading the dirty clanking steamers
—Seeing to the right the Club Nautique
Beyond, the Majestic, haunt of journalists,
And the Hongkong Bank, also the Chartered Bank
Of Australia India and China, and the Banque de l'Indo-
    chine—
And it is not quite as imagination shows us:

J. R. ROWLAND

Telegraph wires hum in a dense grey daylight
Stifling hot; traffic and irritation jam the streets;
Bootblacks nine years old mew at the stranger
With merciless grimace, fight catlike, offer contempt
And filthy postcards. The liftboy turns his back
With a gesture of hatred. It seems a cruel country.

II

Secure in leaves, the lovely trees
Lean from their height upon the square
The sentries idle; everywhere
Soft winds pass and are renewed:
Revolving fans on balconies

Are silent presences, and men
From darkness watch the warmhearted night;
Under the lamps the drivers squat
Naked, in quiet colloquy
By cabaret and gambling-den

Echoes of mortars from the plains
Disturb the city, and the blood
Moves strangely in its moving wood;
Who walks the streets tonight discovers
Obscure conjectures in his veins

He treads along some borderline
Where complicated loyalties stand
In ambush at his either hand:
Questions hidden in the dark
Wait for his unconscious sign

And illdefined uncertainties
Haunt the minatory leaves,
And houses are unlit; and love's
Absence is a breathing wind
Inhabiting the soft-fledged trees.

J. R. ROWLAND

III

Yet, how it catches the imagination—
Especially to walk at night in the streetmarkets
Among shifting crowds: glowing and shadowed flesh
Under the dense white glare of pressurelamps:
Lilyroots octopus and lacquered pigs
Pigeons' heads swallowsnests cocksfeet
Sharks' livers, sunflower and lotus seeds
Charms for potency and against the evil eye
The phrenologist's ghastly cutaway head, the tooth-inlayer
The seller of mirrored sunglasses and artificial eyes
The soupkitchen and the softdrink wagon,
Jade and ivory, mango and durian
Gong and drum, disturbing music,
The onestringed fiddle of beggars, the magic of names
Casting of horoscopes with pebbles and white feathers—

Or by day the streetvendors' tragic minor calls
Passing the window, the clack of their rattles
In the siesta hour, while the fan beats
With measured pulse, and servants gossip
In shady courtyards; or again at night
To ride in a cyclo down avenues of tamarind
And feel the force of each alternate legstroke
Of the grunting driver, who pedals quietly
Touching his little bell, his face in darkness,
Bell that rings and swings, symbol of mystery, promise
Of strangeness and discovery.

FRANCIS WEBB

For My Grandfather

When the ropes droop and loosen, and the gust
Piecemeal upon a widening quietness fails,
Fail breath and spirit; against the bony mast
Work in like skin the frayed and slackened sails.
In the green lull where ribs and keel lie wrecked,
Wrapped in the sodden, enigmatic sand,
Things that ache sunward, seaward, with him locked,
Tug at the rigging of the dead ship-lover's hand.
Though no wind's whitening eloquence may fill
Drowned canvas with the steady bulge of breath,
Doubling for past, for future, are never still
The bones ambiguous with life and death.

Dusk over Bradley's Head: a feeble gull
Whose sinking body is the past at edge
Of form and nothing; here the beautiful
Letona gybes, off the spray-shaken ledge.
And to those years dusk comes but as a rift
In the flesh of sunlight, closed by memory;
Shells stir in the pull of water, lift
Fragile and holy faces to the sky.
My years and yours are scrawled upon this air
Rapped by the gavel of my living breath:
Rather than time upon my wrist I wear
The dial, the four quarters, of your death.

Dawn Wind on the Islands

The needle of dawn has drugged them, life and death,
Stiff and archaic, moulding into one,
Voiceless, having no mission and no path,
Lolling under a heavy head-dress. When
The puppet sun jerks up, there will be no
Convergences: the dead will be the dead,

[Twirled in a yellow . . .

Twirled in a yellow eddy, frail and dull.
These hands of mine that might be stone and snow,
Half bone, half silent fallen dust, will shed
Decay, and flower with the first glittering gull.

Dawn on the wide deserted airstrip swells
And the wind shifts and gains and gathers. If
The point of daylight balances, controls
The sense of life-and-death as on a gaff,
Then dripping it will come, and living—show
From this sea's knotted blue that has no name
While the moon dies on its branches like a leaf;
As coral's whitening belly it will flow
Inland before the sunrise, hang with flame
The tilted freighter breaking on the reef.

Here, where they died, oblivion will burn
The moth-winged bomber's glass and gristle; weirs
Of time will burst, burying them; the sun
Casually mock a cross of stars.
And I have watched them die, wedged fast, below
The tumbling barracks and the yellowing page,
Each day more helpless and more desperate.
At dawn these agonies break loose and grow
Out of the rotted boards, the voices rage:
Cry, cry, but feel—but never forget.

The sun will rise, and with its landward swing
The dead will be the dead, surrendered up
To a dark annexation. Life will hang
Red lights of warning on the crumbling ship.
There will be only life and death. The slow
Roll of the east, the passport of the day
Blazing release, while still this moment lies
Over the island, this. I cannot know
If it is life that wakes, shaking the bay,
Hungry, and circling, and labouring to rise.

FRANCIS WEBB

Morgan's Country

This is Morgan's country: now steady, Bill.
(Stunted and grey, hunted and murderous.)
Squeeze for the first pressure. Shoot to kill.

Five: a star dozing in its cold cavern.
Six: first shuffle of boards in the cold house.
And the sun lagging on seven.

The grey wolf at his breakfast. He cannot think
Why he must make haste, unless because their eyes
Are poison at every well where he might drink.

Unless because their gabbling voices force
The doors of his grandeur—first terror, then only hate.
Now terror again. Dust swarms under the doors.

Ashes drift on the dead-sea shadow of his plate.
Why should he heed them? What to do but kill
When his angel howls, when the sounds reverberate

In the last grey pipe of his brain? At the window sill
A blowfly strums on two strings of air:
Ambush and slaughter tingle against the lull.

But the Cave, his mother, is close beside his chair,
Her sunless face scribbled with cobwebs, bones
Rattling in her throat when she speaks. And there

The stone Look-out, his towering father, leans
Like a splinter from the seamed palm of the plain.
Their counsel of thunder arms him. A threat of rain.

Seven: and a blaze fiercer than the sun.
The wind struggles in the arms of the starved tree,
The temple breaks on a threadbare mat of glass.

Eight: even under the sun's trajectory
This country looks grey, hunted and murderous.

FRANCIS WEBB

A Death at Winson Green

There is a green spell stolen from Birmingham;
Your peering omnibus overlooks the fence,
Or the grey, bobbing lifelines of a tram.
Here, through the small hours, sings our innocence.
Joists, apathetic pillars plot this ward,
Tired timbers wheeze and settle into dust,
We labour, labour: for the treacherous lord
Of time, the dazed historic sunlight, must
Be wheeled in a seizure towards one gaping bed,
Quake like foam on the lip, or lie still as the dead.

Visitors' Day: the graven perpetual smile,
String-bags agape, and pity's laundered glove.
The last of the heathens shuffles down the aisle,
Dark glass to a beauty which we hate and love.
Our empires rouse against this ancient fear,
Longsufferings, anecdotes, levelled at our doom;
Mine-tracks of old allegiance, prying here,
Perplex the sick man raving in his room.
Outside, a shunting engine hales from bed
The reminiscent feast-day, long since dead.

Noon reddens, trader birds deal cannily
With Winson Green, and the slouch-hatted sun
Gapes at windows netted in wire, and we
Like early kings with book and word cast down
Realities from our squared electric shore.
Two orderlies are whistling-in the spring;
Doors slam; and a man is dying at the core
Of triumph won. As a tattered, powerful wing
The screen bears out his face against the bed,
Silver, derelict, rapt, and almost dead.

Evening gropes out of colour; yet we work
To cleanse our shore from limpet histories;
Traffic and factory-whistle turn berserk;
Inviolate, faithful as a saint he lies.

Twilight itself breaks up, the venal ship,
Upon the silver integrity of his face.
No bread shall tempt that fine, tormented lip.
Let shadow switch to light—he holds his place.
Unmarked, unmoving, from the gaping bed
Towards birth he labours, honour, almost dead.

The wiry cricket moiling at his loom
Debates a themeless project with dour night,
The sick man raves beside me in his room;
I sleep as a child, rouse up as a child might.
I cannot pray; that fine lip prays for me
With every gasp at breath; his burden grows
Heavier as all earth lightens, and all sea.
Time crouches, watching, near his face of snows.
He is all life, thrown on the gaping bed
Blind, silent, in a trance, and shortly, dead.

Harry

It's the day for writing that letter, if one is able,
And so the striped institutional shirt is wedged
Between this holy holy chair and table.
He has purloined paper, he has begged and cadged
The bent institutional pen,
The ink. And our droll old men
Are darting constantly where he weaves his sacrament.

Sacrifice? Propitiation? All are blent
In the moron's painstaking fingers—so painstaking.
His vestments our giddy yarns of the firmament,
Women, gods, electric trains, and our remaking
Of all known worlds—but not yet
Has our giddy alphabet
Perplexed his priestcraft and spilled the cruet of innocence.

[We have been plucked . . .

We have been plucked from the world of commonsense,
Fondling between our hands some shining loot,
Wife, mother, beach, fisticuffs, eloquence,
As the lank tree cherishes every distorted shoot.
What queer shards we could steal
Shaped him, realer than the Real:
But it is no goddess of ours guiding the fingers and the thumb.

She cries: *Ab aeterno ordinata sum.*
He writes to the woman, this lad who will never marry.
One vowel and the thousand laborious serifs will come
To this pudgy Christ, and the old shape of Mary.
Before seasonal pelts and the thin
Soft tactile underskin
Of air were stretched across earth, they have sported and are
    one.

Was it then at this altar-stone the mind was begun?
The image besieges our Troy. Consider the sick
Convulsions of movement, and the featureless baldy sun
Insensible—sparing that compulsive nervous tic.
Before life, the fantastic succession,
An imbecile makes his confession,
Is filled with the Word unwritten, has almost genuflected.

Because the wise world has for ever and ever rejected
Him and because your children would scream at the sight
Of his mongol mouth stained with food, he has resurrected
The spontaneous thought retarded and infantile Light.
Transfigured with him we stand
Among walls of the no-man's-land
While he licks the soiled envelope with lover's caress.

Directing it to the House of no known address.

Angels' Weather

Watching Rushcutters' bright bayful of masts and coloured
    keels,
Half-sensing Dufy's muse walking on that gull, sail
And cobalt sky reflecting surface,
I open my senses to the gift of it and hear
The yacht club telecommunication paging
A Mr Fairweather over the water;
Watch gulls wheeling one after the other
After another with sustenance in its beak.
Frantic as white sharks they thresh the blue waters of the air.
Perched on a dory a shag replete
Flaps dry and stretches out its black umbrella wings.
On the mud-flat's rank solarium
A few grounded parent birds are teaching their young
To walk tip-web-toe,
Heads pointed up at the sun-mote
Swarms of gnat-fry,
Fishing the citron-scented shallows of noon.

Passing are pattern stockinged girls
With old dogs and strollers full of family.
Prim seated or grass floored the sun imbibers,
Some still hung from last night's
Vinegary round of dark: the White Lady presiding
Somewhere near the tolling two o'clock till,
Honing her crescent. Now only
The grass poking its tongues out at our fears;
The coral trees' crimson beaks of bloom pecking the blue.
Above the doughy park's arena of tiger-striped
And cougar-charcoaled athletes
A murmuration of applause for no-one in particular
From the immense and yellow foliaged
Fig leafing through the wind;
Spectator of the sportive weather.
Olympiads of effort are stored, restored
Within that echo-memory of clapping leaf.

[Now we are all . . .

145

Now we are all sun lovers, steaming in tweeds and
      combinations.
Be it upon our own heads
This blessed incontinent surrendering
To the open handed noon broadcasting silence
And the bright winged seeds of peace which find their nest
In an evening of visionary trees.

from *Letters to Live Poets*

XVI

Our street is known as the street of widows.
Seven of its residents, including my mother,
have survived their husbands.
But two of the seven have weak hearts.
They listen to themselves living.

This morning at 4 am a storm broke overhead.
So fierce it was, a cloudburst.
The pelting wet and cracking thunder
skinned me of sleep. I lay sickly
with a dry mouth and knotted gut,
hearing the sizzling crack of lightning's javelins.
I had a target
throbbing in my heart.
I thought of the bereaved women

and of my wife beside me
whose quiet, innate calm
would outbluff any storm.
'Grant her a winner's heart
and residual courage,' I prayed
in melodramatic silence
between thunder claps.

The huge wash of rain came through
the kitchen's roof, soaking the floor.
The electric point spat and stank
and the fire worry returned.
What would I save first,
clothes or manuscripts?
The latter would not buy me a shirt.
I saw us all barefooted in the chilly
streaming gutter under the dribbling
pine, water and fire contending
at dead of night in the morning,
time of sick dreams and lonely vigils.
But *the poet is the true stealer of fire*
I told myself, doubtingly.

Now in the dull light of the washed-out
day the old and the young women
of the street rehearse their roles
of mothers, wives, survivors.
I alone am the witnessing male
of their floured and peeled existence,
the sole drone immune to their stinging gaze.
Their sunshine squeaks and twitches
from the electric machines. The ordinary,
distorted voices of the announcers drone and bleat;
the hogwash of muzak slops
and spills about their doughy ears.

Everywhere but in this faded
street is life. Everywhere
is living. Is this street.
And the pines
drip with doves. Seagulls
spot the biscuit coloured beach
with white. The rain-pocked sands
suck the wet down to the base of
rock. The holiday kids crouch
in shelters, eating chips, combing
hair, smelling each other's transistors,
their sex bursting from faded denim.

[Thinking of them . . .

BRUCE BEAVER

Thinking of them all the long, wet morning
I'm almost glad I was born middle-aged.
I process raisins from the sourest grapes
and spit the pips into the morning's maw.

R. F. BRISSENDEN

The Death of Damiens *or* l'Après-midi des lumières

Place de Grève, Paris, March 28 1757

The man's left leg
Is torn away at last.
It drags behind the stallion
Over the cobbles.

The waiting crowd
Packed like cattle into the square
Clap, roar and stamp their feet.
The man kisses the crucifix.

From a high window
Casanova and his friend,
Six-time-a-night Tiretta,
Watch with their women.

Immaculate in white,
Henri Sanson with glowing pincers
Plucks out a lump of flesh
From the man's bared chest.

R. F. BRISSENDEN

His five assistant executioners
Moving like priests
Pour in the boiling oil,
The molten lead.

The stench fills the square.
The lathered horses,
Jerking under the whip,
Strain at the heavy cables.

Tiretta, unbuttoned,
Lifts from behind the long silk skirt
Of the Pope's niece.
The other leg comes off.

Robert Damiens screams.
Casanova, cupping the warm young breast
Of Mademoiselle de la Meure,
Turns her virginal head away.

'Animals, animals!' he mutters
Smiling. 'Look, my dear:
The dying madman's hair
Has all gone white.'

PETER PORTER

Sydney Cove, 1788

The Governor loves to go mapping—round and round
The inlets of the Harbour in his pinnace.
He fingers a tree-fern, sniffs the ground

[And hymns it . . .

And hymns it with a unison of feet—
We march to church and executions. No-one,
Even Banks, could match the flora of our fleet.

Grog from Madeira reminds us most of home,
More than the pork and British weevils do.
On a diet of flour, your hair comes out in your comb.

A seaman who tried to lie with a native girl
Ran off when he smelt her fatty hide.
Some say these oysters are the sort for pearls.

Green shoots of the Governor's wheat have browned.
A box of bibles was washed up today,
The chaplain gave them to two methodists. Ross found

A convict selling a baby for a jug of rum.
Those black hills which wrestle with
The rain are called Blue Mountains. Come

Genocide or Jesus we can't work this land.
The sun has framed it for our moralists
To dry the bones of forgers in the sand.

We wake in the oven of its cloudless sky,
Already the blood-encircled sun is up.
Mad sharks swim in the convenient sea.

The Governor says we mustn't land a man
Or woman with gonorrhoea. Sound felons only
May leave their bodies in a hangman's land.

Where all is novel, the only rule's explore.
Amelia Levy and Elizabeth Fowles spent the night
With Corporal Plowman and Corporal Winxstead for

A shirt apiece. These are our home concerns.
The cantor curlew sings the surf asleep.
The moon inducts the lovers in the ferns.

PETER PORTER

The Last of England

It's quiet here among the haunted tenses:
Dread Swiss germs pass the rabbit's throat,
Chemical rain in its brave green hat
Drinks at a South Coast Bar, the hedgehog
Preens on nylon, we dance in Tyrolean
Drag whose mothers were McGregors,
Exiled seas fill every cubit of the bay.

Sailing away from ourselves, we feel
The gentle tug of water at the quay—
Language of the liberal dead speaks
From the soil of Highgate, tears
Show a great water table is intact.
You cannot leave England, it turns
A planet majestically in the mind.

An Exequy

In wet May, in the months of change,
In a country you wouldn't visit, strange
Dreams pursue me in my sleep,
Black creatures of the upper deep—
Though you are five months dead, I see
You in guilt's iconography,
Dear Wife, lost beast, beleaguered child,
The stranded monster with the mild
Appearance, whom small waves tease,
(Andromeda upon her knees
In orthodox deliverance)
And you alone of pure substance,
The unformed form of life, the earth
Which Piero's brushes brought to birth
For all to greet as myth, a thing
Out of the box of imagining.

[This introduction . . .

PETER PORTER

This introduction serves to sing
Your mortal death as Bishop King
Once hymned in tetrametric rhyme
His young wife, lost before her time;
Though he lived on for many years
His poem each day fed new tears
To that unreaching spot, her grave,
His lines a baroque architrave
The Sunday poor with bottled flowers
Would by-pass in their mourning hours,
Esteeming ragged natural life
('Most dearly loved, most gentle wife'),
Yet, looking back when at the gate
And seeing grief in formal state
Upon a sculpted angel group,
Were glad that men of god could stoop

To give the dead a public stance
And freeze them in their mortal dance.
The words and faces proper to
My misery are private—you
Would never share your heart with those
Whose only talent's to suppose,
Nor from your final childish bed
Raise a remote confessing head—
The channels of our lives are blocked,
The hand is stopped upon the clock,
No-one can say why hearts will break
And marriages are all opaque:
A map of loss, some posted cards,
The living house reduced to shards,
The abstract hell of memory,
The pointlessness of poetry—
These are the instances which tell
Of something which I know full well,
I owe a death to you—one day
The time will come for me to pay
When your slim shape from photographs
Stands at my door and gently asks
If I have any work to do
Or will I come to bed with you.

O scala enigmatica,
I'll climb up to that attic where
The curtain of your life was drawn
Some time between despair and dawn—
I'll never know with what halt steps
You mounted to this plain eclipse
But each stair now will station me
A black responsbility
And point me to that shut-down room,
'This be your due appointed tomb.'

I think of us in Italy:
Gin-and-chianti-fuelled, we
Move in a trance through Paradise,
Feeding at last our starving eyes,
Two people of the English blindness
Doing each masterpiece the kindness
Of discovering it—from Baldovinetti
To Venice's most obscure jetty.
A true unfortunate traveller, I
Depend upon your nurse's eye
To pick the altars where no Grinner
Puts us off our tourists' dinner
And in hotels to bandy words
With Genevan girls and talking birds,
To wear your feet out following me
To night's end and true amity,
And call my rational fear of flying
A paradigm of Holy Dying—
And, oh my love, I wish you were
Once more with me, at night somewhere
In narrow streets applauding wines,
The moon above the Apennines
As large as logic and the stars,
Most middle-aged of avatars,
As bright as when they shone for truth
Upon untried and avid youth.

[The rooms and days . . .

The rooms and days we wandered through
Shrink in my mind to one—there you
Lie quite absorbed by peace—the calm
Which life could not provide is balm
In death. Unseen by me, you look
Past bed and stairs and half-read book
Eternally upon your home,
The end of pain, the left alone.
I have no friend, or intercessor,
No psychopomp or true confessor
But only you who know my heart
In every cramped and devious part—
Then take my hand and lead me out,
The sky is overcast by doubt,
The time has come, I listen for
Your words of comfort at the door,
O guide me through the shoals of fear—
'Fürchte dich nicht, ich bin bei dir.'

Non piangere, Liù

A card comes to tell you
you should report
to have your eyes tested.

But your eyes melted in the fire
and the only tears, which soon dried,
fell in the chapel.

Other things still come—
invoices, subscription renewals,
shiny plastic cards promising credit—
not much for a life spent
in the service of reality.

You need answer none of them.
Nor my asking you for one drop
of succour in my own hell.

Do not cry, I tell myself,
the whole thing is a comedy
and comedies end happily.

The fire will come out of the sun
and I shall look in the heart of it.

'In the New World happiness is allowed'

No, in the New World, happiness is enforced.
It leans your neck over the void and the only
recourse is off to Europe and the crowded hearts,
a helplessness of pasta and early closing days,
lemons glowing through the blood of Acre.

Is it the glaze of galvanism—why are there
so many madmen in the street? O, my countrymen,
success is an uncle leaving you his fruit farm.
The end of the world with deep-freezes, what if
your memories are only made of silence?

In one year he emptied the sea of a ton of fish.
He wasn't one to look at the gardens of Greenslopes
and wish they were the verdure of the Casentino.
Living with the world's reserves of ores,
no wonder our ruined Virgils become democrats.

Masturbation has been known in Europe too
and among the gentiles. Why did nobody say
that each successful man needs the evidence
of a hundred failures? There is weekend leave
from Paradise, among the caravanning angels.

[Here's a vision . . .

Here's a vision may be painted on a wall:
a man and a boy are eating with an aborigine
in a boat; the sun turns up the tails of fish
lying beside the oars; the boy wipes surreptitiously
the bottle passed him by the black man.

Rain strums the library roof. The talk tonight
is 'Voluntary Euthanasia'. Trying to be classical
can break your heart. Depression long persisted in
becomes despair. Forgive me, friends and relatives,
for this unhappiness, I was away from home.

R. A. SIMPSON

Landscape

The river is a thought that pours slowly
Down from nowhere, and soon it disappears
Beyond my view and apprehension.
This landscape also has its moving fears.

Here is a mind, and though I look at it
I cannot tell just what it thinks or knows,
Believe it calm as sunlight wakes through clouds,
But feel uncertain as a cloud-thought grows.

Although the rocks are firm, here nothing lasts
Because a text-book tells me that the hills
Were monolithic like a faith, then rain
And servitude, the days of finer wills

Attacked all strength and left pebbles and weeds
To waste. But if a landscape had a voice
And nihilistic words, it might explain
How much is accident and how much choice.

R. A. SIMPSON

All Friends Together

A Survey of Present-day Australian Poetry

Charles and Bruce, Geoff and Ron and Nancy
May publish books this year: some hope they won't.
Tom and Les, Robert, Nan and John—
We live our lives quietly using words
And write of dragons and birds: we are our critics.
Asia, of course, is waiting, but somewhere else.

Max and Rod and Les, and someone else,
Are writing well, and so are Charles and John.
Who would have thought they knew so many words.
Who would have thought this country had such critics.
Mary may come good some day—she won't,
Of course. And yet we may all hear from Nancy.

Nan and Don are better now than Nancy.
Robert, too, writes well for all the critics—
And did you see that latest thing by John?
Nothing queer—the 'queers' are somewhere else
Painting paintings. And all our poems won't
Be anything but normal. We know our words

And buy anthologies to read our words—
David, Robert, Ron and Alex and Nancy.
And did you choke upon that thing by John?
Wasps and grass, magpies and something else
Have often made us write: I'm sure they won't
Seem overdone; they always please the critics.

The critics know (of course, we are the critics)
The qualities of Max and Geoff and Nancy.
And so we carry on with Charles and John,
Tom and Alex, Robert, and someone else—
Big thoughts about a myth, and simple words.
Perhaps you think we'll stop, and yet we won't.

[Sometimes I think . . .

Sometimes I think we'll stop, and yet we won't—
John and David, Bruce and Ron and Nancy,
Robert and Les, Rod and someone else,
Who love the words of friends, and please the critics
With neat anthologies and simple words—
Geoff and Max, Charles and Gwen and John.

Sometimes I think that Nancy, Don and John
And someone else are neither poets nor critics:
They won't like that. We only have our words.

Visit to the Museum

My children haul me there
To see the animals—
Phar Lap, bones of elephants,
Spiders pinned so finally
The room has a bad taste
A boy's excitement overruns.

I keep looking at exits
While fumbling to tell
Why the monkey resembles life.
My daughter's sad.
My son points to the part that's rude,
And the monkey is oblivion.

My daughter wants to know
If people, when they die,
Are sometimes kept like animals.
We laugh.
A waxy attendant near the door
Reads behind glass.

R. A. SIMPSON

My children leave me for a leopard;
I'm suddenly aware
Of a room where dead friends stand
Encased for only me to view.
I drown through glass to them
Till rescued by a shout.

Sorrow and regret remain
Too abstract for those friends
Who never looked for a museum,
Even in me. I live with exhibits,
Rows and rows of question marks
On which I cannot hang my coat.

BRUCE DAWE

First Corinthians at the Crossroads

When I was a blonde I
walked as a blonde I
talked as a blonde;
but now that I have become
a brunette I have put away my
blonding lotion, farewell Kim Novak
and the statuesque Nordic
me: a touching scene truly . . .
We lingered like old lovers
who cannot quite believe
the evidence of their eyes.
'It is all over, honey-bun, alas,' said disconsolate
eyebrows being terribly
brave.

['Toujours, toujours,' . . .

BRUCE DAWE

'Toujours, toujours,' sang lips that had
tasted their last Tango, while
onward onward into an everlasting
brunette dusk we moved to confront,
with the new dawn's rising
over a wasteland of depilatory and
Beauty-Mask, O
brave new world . . .

Drifters

One day soon he'll tell her it's time to start packing,
and the kids will yell 'Truly?' and get wildly excited for no
    reason,
and the brown kelpie pup will start dashing about, tripping
    everyone up,
and she'll go out to the vegetable-patch and pick all the green
    tomatoes from the vines,
and notice how the oldest girl is close to tears because she was
    happy here,
and how the youngest girl is beaming because she wasn't.
And the first thing she'll put on the trailer will be the bottling-
    set she never unpacked from Grovedale,
and when the loaded ute bumps down the drive past the
    blackberry-canes with their last shrivelled fruit,
she won't even ask why they're leaving this time, or where
    they're heading for
—she'll only remember how, when they came here,
she held out her hands bright with berries,
the first of the season, and said:
'Make a wish, Tom, make a wish.'

BRUCE DAWE

The Not-so-good Earth

For a while there we had 25-inch Chinese peasant families
famishing in comfort on the 25-inch screen
and even Uncle Billy whose eyesight's going fast
by hunching up real close to the convex glass
could just about make them out—the riot scene
in the capital city for example
he saw that better than anything, using the contrast knob
to bring them up dark—all those screaming faces
and bodies going under the horses' hooves—he did a terrific
    job
on that bit, not so successful though
on the quieter parts where they're just starving away
digging for roots in the not-so-good earth
cooking up a mess of old clay
and coming out with all those Confucian analects
to everybody's considerable satisfaction
(if I remember rightly Grandmother dies
with naturally a suspenseful break in the action
for a full symphony orchestra plug for Craven A
neat as a whistle probably damn glad
to be quit of the whole gang with their marvellous patience.)
We never did find out how it finished up . . . Dad
at this stage tripped over the main lead in the dark
hauling the whole set down smack on its inscrutable face,
wiping out in a blue flash and curlicue of smoke
600 million Chinese without a trace . . .

BRUCE DAWE

Homecoming

All day, day after day, they're bringing them home,
they're picking them up, those they can find, and bringing
   them home,
they're bringing them in, piled on the hulls of Grants, in
   trucks, in convoys,
they're zipping them up in green plastic bags,
they're tagging them now in Saigon, in the mortuary coolness
they're giving them names, they're rolling them out of
the deep-freeze lockers—on the tarmac at Tan Son Nhut
the noble jets are whining like hounds,
they are bringing them home
—curly-heads, kinky-hairs, crew-cuts, balding non-coms
—they're high, now, high and higher, over the land, the
   steaming *chow mein*,
their shadows are tracing the blue curve of the Pacific
with sorrowful quick fingers, heading south, heading east,
home, home, home—and the coasts swing upward, the old
   ridiculous curvatures
of earth, the knuckled hills, the mangrove-swamps, the desert
   emptiness . . .
in their sterile housing they tilt towards these like skiers
—taxiing in, on the long runways, the howl of their
   homecoming rises
surrounding them like their last moments (the mash, the
   splendour)
then fading at length as they move
on to small towns where dogs in the frozen sunset
raise muzzles in mute salute,
and on to cities in whose wide web of suburbs
telegrams tremble like leaves from a wintering tree
and the spider grief swings in his bitter geometry
—they're bringing them home, now, too late, too early.

The Falling Sickness

The foliage of light begins to wither
Into a dark discontinuity,
And in that darkness now I bring together
A pattern of disorder, tenuously:

Dim squares of light and shade, this music and these voices.
Under the skin and flesh my fingers feel
The fine erratic structure that encases
The focus of all movement. I lie still.

Now in a little while this world that I
Could shut out with a hand will take its sway
Till I have misremembered that outcry
And stagger forward into yesterday.

The Compound

Somewhere inside something is walking about,
Shuffling, shadowy, slipping from place to place,
With not much being, and no face:
It wants to get out.

Nothing is peering into its gloom but walls,
Sentient layers crowded course on course—
To baffle seduction, to block force;
To pad the blind beast's falls.

Somewhere inside, it limps like a wounded creature,
Pauses to lick its wounds, goes off, and on:
Wherever the walls' eyes focus, it is gone:
It is their nature.

[It growls: though hardly . . .

EVAN JONES

It growls: though hardly existing, it is there—
Walls keep intact: they shift
At touch, grow against strain and rift
Into that glass-faced shelter where
Insufferable bareness is able to shamble bare.

Language, talk to me

Language talk to me, language
tell me what I know
after forty years—
language, will you show
the way out of the labyrinth
to me, myopic, slow
and singular as when
I fell in love with you
twenty odd years ago?

Language talk to me, language,
while I listen for
the wheezing snuffling clumping
of the Minotaur:
now from your endless store
recruit a devotee who
on this illegible shore
lost, without a clue,
turns as ever to you.

Language talk to me, language
teach me what to say
in the face of disaster,
in the height of hope,
as things fall away.
Mother-tongue, lingua franca,
all that anyone knows,
bring me, kindly bring me
to a perfect close.

VIVIAN SMITH

At an Exhibition
of Historical Paintings, Hobart

The sadness in the human visage stares
out of these frames, out of these distant eyes;
the static bodies painted without love
that only lack of talent could disguise.

Those bland receding hills are too remote
where the quaint natives squat with awkward calm.
One carries a kangaroo like a worn toy,
his axe alert with emphasized alarm.

Those nearer woollen hills are now all streets;
even the water in the harbour's changed.
Much is alike and yet a slight precise
disparity seems intended and arranged—

as in that late pink terrace's façade.
How neat the houses look. How clean each brick.
One cannot say they look much older now,
but somehow more themselves, less accurate.

And see the pride in this expansive view:
churches, houses, farms, a prison tower;
a grand gesture like wide-open arms
showing the artist's trust, his clumsy power.

And this much later vision, grander still:
the main street sedate carriages unroll
towards the inappropriate, tentative mountain:
a flow of lines the artist can't control—

the foreground nearly breaks out of its frame
the streets end so abruptly in the water . . .
But how some themes return. A whaling ship.
The last natives. Here that silent slaughter

[is really not . . .

is really not prefigured or avoided.
One merely sees a profile, a full face,
a body sitting stiffly in a chair:
the soon-forgotten absence of a race . . .

Album pieces: bowls of brown glazed fruit . . .
I'm drawn back yet again to those few studies
of native women whose long floral dresses
made them first aware of their own bodies.

History has made artists of all these
painters who lack energy and feature.
But how some gazes cling. Around the hall
the pathos of the past, the human creature.

FAY ZWICKY

Summer Pogrom

Spade-bearded Grandfather, squat Lenin
In the snows of Donna Buang.
Your bicycle a wiry crutch, nomadic homburg
Alien, black, correct. Beneath, the curt defiant
Filamented eye. Does it count the dead
Between the Cossack horses' legs in Kovno?

Those dead who sleep in me, me dry
In a garden veiled with myrtle and oleander,
Desert snows that powder memory's track
Scoured by burning winds from eastern rocks,
Flushing the lobes of mind,
Fat white dormant flowrets.

FAY ZWICKY

Aggressive under dappled shade, girl in a glove;
Collins Street in autumn,
Mirage of clattering crowds: Why don't you speak English?
I don't understand, *I don't understand!*
Sei nicht so ein Dummerchen, nobody cares.
Not for you the upreared hooves of Nikolai,
Eat your icecream, Kleine, *may his soul rot,*
These are good days.

Flared candles; the gift of children; love,
Need fulfilled, a name it has to have—how else to feel?
A radiance in the garden, the Electrolux man chats,
Cosy spectre of the afternoon's decay.
My eye his eye, the snows of Kovno cover us.
Is that my son bloodied against Isaac the Baker's door?

The tepid river's edge, reeds creak, rats' nests fold and quiver,
My feet sink in sand; the children splash and call, sleek
Little satyrs diamond-eyed reined to summer's roundabout,
Hiding from me. Must I excavate you,
Agents of my death? Hushed snows are deep, the
Dead lie deep in me.

DAVID MALOUF

The Year of the Foxes

When I was ten, my mother, having sold
her old fox-fur (a ginger red, bone-jawed
Magda Lupescu
of a fox that on her arm played
dead, cunningly dangled
a lean and tufted paw),

[decided there was . . .

decided there was money to be made
from foxes, and bought via
the columns of the *Courier Mail* a whole
pack of them; they hung from penny hooks
in our panelled sitting-room, trailed from the backs
of chairs; and Brisbane ladies, rather
the worse for war, drove up in taxis wearing
a G.I. on their arm,
and rang at our front door.

I slept across the hall, at night hearing
their thin cold cry. I dreamed the dangerous spark
of their eyes, brushes aflame
in our fur-hung, nomadic
tent in the suburbs, the dark fox-stink of them,
cornered in their holes
and turning . . .
             Among my mother's show-pieces:
Noritaki teacups, tall hock glasses
with stems like barley-sugar,
goldleaf demitasses—
the foxes, row upon row, thin-nosed, prick-eared,
dead.
     The cry of hounds
was lost behind mirror-glass,
where ladies with silken snoods and finger-nails
of chinese lacquer red,
fastened a limp paw;
went down in their high heels
to the warm soft bitumen, wearing at throat
and elbow the rare spoils
of '44: old foxes, rusty red like dried-up wounds,
and a G.I. escort.

DAVID MALOUF

A Charm against the Dumps

Shoo! be far off! fly
on owl's-wing feather-duster
be sucked into the belly
of Hoover go swirling
down plug-hole you

Bumbo lord of the dumps lord
of toothache and hay fever
of thumbnail by hammer
blackened spent matches
nose-bleeds razor-nicks

and all you left-handed
dialers of wrong numbers
stammerers stumblers
and tittle-tats madcap
demons at the wheel

the charm against your sullen
mischief is sneezing
at sunshine cold keys
slipped between skin and sweater
or counting to ten

but best of all Bumbo
lord of the dumps is shouting
so loud under the blankets
you tumble out ears ringing
the right side of the bed

CHRIS WALLACE-CRABBE

A Wintry Manifesto

It was the death of Satan first of all,
The knowledge that earth holds though kingdoms fall,
    Inured us to a stoic resignation,
    To make the most of a shrunken neighbourhood;

And what we draw on was not gold or fire,
No cross, not cloven hoof about the pyre,
    But painful, plain, contracted observations:
    The gesture of a hand, dip of a bough

Or seven stubborn words drawn close together
As a hewn charm against the shifting weather.
    Our singing was intolerably sober
    Mistrusting every trill of artifice.

Whatever danced on needle-points, we knew
That we had forged the world we stumbled through
    And, if a stripped wind howled through sighing alleys,
    Built our own refuge in a flush of pride

Knowing that all our gifts were for construction—
Timber to timber groined in every section—
    And knowing, too, purged of the sense of evil,
    These were the walls our folly would destroy.

We dreamed, woke, doubted, wept for fading stars
And then projected brave new avatars,
    Triumphs of reason. Yet a whole dimension
    Had vanished from the chambers of the mind,

And paramount among the victims fled,
Shrunken and pale, the grim king of the dead;
    Withdrawn to caverns safely beyond our sounding
    He waits as a Pretender for his call,

Which those who crave him can no longer give.
Men are the arbiters of how they live,
    And, stooped by millstones of authority,
    They welcome tyrants in with open arms.

Now in the shadows of unfriendly trees
We number leaves, discern faint similes
    And learn to praise whatever is imperfect
    As the true breeding-ground for honesty,

Finding our heroism in rejection
Of bland Utopias and of thieves' affection:
    Our greatest joy to mark an outline truly
    And know the piece of earth on which we stand.

An Allegiance

Drab skyline, yellowing papers, a fat land,
To these I am drawn
Tightly and unreasonably because
I was born here,
        I am shaped by
These watercoloured hills and plains,
These delicate straggling creeks,
This paper blankness
On which all writing still is to be done,
Each line of meaning still to be inscribed
In joy,
        in labour generating joy.

CHRIS WALLACE-CRABBE

Introspection

Have you ever seen a mind
thinking?
It is like an old cow
trying to get through the pub door
carrying a guitar in its mouth;
old habits keep breaking in
on the job in hand;
it keeps wanting
to do something else:
like having a bit of a graze
for example,
or galumphing round the paddock
or being a cafe musician
with a beret and a moustache.
But if she just keeps trying
the old cow, avec guitar,
will be through that door
as easy as pie
but she won't know how it was done.
It's harder with a piano.

Have you ever heard the havoc
of remembering?
It is like asking
the local plumber
in to explore a disused well;
down he goes on a twisting rope,
his cloddy boots
bumping against
that slimed brickwork,
and when he arrives at bottom
in the smell of darkness,
with a splash of jet black water
he grasps a huge fish,
slices it open
with his clasp-knife
and finds a gold coin inside

which slips
out of his fingers
back into the unformed unseeing,
never to be found again.

Old Men during a Fall of Government

Mortality grows all over them
like a field of flowers

Their bodies are geologically
pre-Cambrian or such,

gullies and dingles everywhere,
erosion, moraines:

you can glimpse the original outline
the colour of reminiscence

before their eyes retired
behind these fleshy blinds.

The political bloodfield thunders
but its runnel of destruction

does not even reach them.
They are unproductive paddocks

out back of nowhere.
Look at those veins, like poppies,

and that once-ripe hair,
a thin scurf of snowdrops,

and the tears.

LEWIS PACKER

Homecoming
In memoriam: George South

The bird a nest, the spider a web, man friendship.
wm. blake

There will be a homecoming. There will.
  Our cavern is not forever.
Roar of sunlight on the naked eye,
the snapped chain, the dance,
the unexpected bride and the absolute honey
in the restored garden,
these will be yours, will be mine, and together.

Though some of us are not here to tell it,
are away, interpreting a colder night
   where no voice touches them
but the slow, sad, single note of themselves
keening among snuffed stars,
there will be a homecoming. There will.

One walked a crooked city with me, so simple
he carried teddy bears to orphanages,
and laughed right back at the laughter.
  It burns me he is not here.
  He knew
about poems, and children, and fruit-flies.
He stuttered. He was curly,
and brothered me once with half his money.
  He learned the music of India,
then switched himself off
      with a spoonful of tablets
alone in our haunted house,
being sick from naming ghosts. He was my friend,
simply,
  a dove beside a tiger,
and he will have his homecoming.

I call him to be ambassador
for all absent, broken on the wheel of hard praising
where children plead in napalm robes,
            and to tell him:
though their bodies are burned as casually as chips,
it will be all right, George. It will be all right.
There will be a homecoming.
There will.

And at that homecoming, George,
you will have apples again, your girl to share them
unhurried on a wide bed, and no more grief for children
            tossed on the bayonets of the deaf,
to make you leap into God's blindness.
All our rivers will run clean,
and there will be good bread and invitations where
only blood is now, and the tillers weeping.
            Time is merely a wheel, my friend;
            so no loss endures forever.

Your death, flung at me as
indifferently as a newspaper, was a scald I wore
five years, railing at it drunk, past cop cars
cruising like killer whales in our Sargasso.
That is over. Over. I am healed
by a quieter wine.
                    Yes. Into my broken mouth
is poured the wine of renewal.

It will be poured for you,
and for all who drag their exile wounds around,
through and through the black gates.
It will be poured into birth upon birth until
the lover puts down his murdering high,
            the visionary turns back his eyes
from the asylum wall,
                        head ablaze with blessings,
and a tongue to fire the streets.

                        [And if spittle is . . .

LEWIS PACKER

And if spittle is all his payment for saying,
if all men stone him as a displeasing mirror,
still he will open his face, accepting no hideout,
        because he is forever,
and his, his, is the homecoming.

The green shoot will break the rock. It will flower;
our tombs of loss will shatter,
and there will be a homecoming.
There will.
        There will.
                There will.

THOMAS W. SHAPCOTT

The Trees: a Convict Monologue

1
I move sharp, not too fancy or nice—a lurch,
a curse, a getaway. They called me mudsplash
but I was quicker: my eyes have been everywhere
two jumps before you.
What a laugh to be flicked in for passing forged currency!
I'm still laughing—rather laugh than dance, I tell you.
The others were fools on the convictship, but I rubbed close in
just for the mansmell, to remind myself we were still living.
My guts ache most for the people-breath of streets:
while I was free I never left the city but once—
shit, the stink of countryside! air to blast your snotholes
fill you full of bush and breeze and bloody distances.
The only good thing was it taught me, then,
that even air is special: one gulp and you know
you are home in my lovely broken-mouthed slut city.

2
I got used to chains. There were always others
near enough to hit and to hurt and to squeeze in to;
I tell you I was sharper than the rest, I was patient.
And I was high on the good list, none of your grumble
and blood. I joked like the city,
I made them laugh and remember—but no commerce named;
in two years I negotiated my sentence for a good kitchen,
with a wench there one of the prettier bitches.
I used her. And the master was, well, I had hopes.

3
But, after the barracks and sturdy crush of quarters, the open
unnerved me, I had not planned on that—the just nothing
of hills, hollows ridges. Nobody told me trees watched,
connived, were not still, were never still.
They rubbed, they grew blisters like their blistered leaves.
At first, night-time, listen, something about aloneness,
but later, even at day, it was voices no one could live with,
not human: earth, decay, silences. That was it—silence
speaking to me. I did not scream. Rubbing. Suddenly
to wake trapped, held down in nothing but emptiness
and to run screaming, voice rattling to drown that foreignness
till the cavities of the head were cities of yell myself myself
all through the too bright moonsilence and the hallways.
And then ropes and then whips beat me sensible.
I am recovered. I will cut down every tree,
every one. I will be invincible.

June Fugue

1
Where shall we go? where shall we go?
—We shall go to the Museum
What shall we see? is there lots to see?
—We shall see rooms full of treasures
I want to see jewels and costumes
pharaohs and mummies
—We shall spend hours among relics
   We shall be able to look hard
     at the blackened wrists of mummies.

THOMAS W. SHAPCOTT

2

Do you remember that June day we drove into the mountains
we sang together all the songs from *Salad Days* and *My Fair
    Lady?*
—Shall we sing those songs now? Remember them?
No I was thinking of the mountains   the walking track
through that patch of rainforest
—And when we reached the sunlight
        I picked you an everlasting daisy.
You were always bringing me things.

3

Do you remember the images the children said
'Why don't trees have two legs?'
'Daddy look at the broken moon'
'Mummy come in come inside you'll get the dark
            all over you.'
Children are so unalike.
They all draw bodies of sticks and daisies and circles.

4

Where is that human hand? where is the Egyptian Mummy?
I'm sick of stuffed birds like the cat brought in.
—It is a hand small as yours   but very dark
        dried out   a bundle of sticks
Where is it now show me   show me

5

The attendants are bored   the children stop
and then laugh as they move on   it is nothing
how shall I tell them the curse is true?
that out in the sunlight their shoulders are fingered
that already the things they bring in as Everlastings
have the smell of Museums   that once having drawn the
    circle
you will   get the dark all over you

THOMAS W. SHAPCOTT

The Blue Paisley Shirt

My friend the blue paisley shirt is always assured
like eyes that crinkle up with goodhumour
he walks in the room
and is made welcome.   Like laughing eyes
he seems a multiplicity of welcomes.
I bought my blue paisley shirt to make me friendly
to offer the grin of my shirt, its brisk handshake.
It is a dark blue, and the paisley white curls even its toes.
When I first put it on I felt good, so
this afternoon I walked into the crowded room
and my wife's deodorant under my armpits strewed petals
as I moved.   Surely you saw me?   Saw me standing
a middle-ageing fool in white jeans and last season's sideburns
my face made naked above its shirt of skulls?

RANDOLPH STOW

Dust

'Enough,' she said. But the dust still rained around her:
over her living room (hideous, autumnal)
dropping its small defiance.
                              The clock turned green.

She spurned her broom and took a train. The neighbours
have heard nothing.

Jungles, deserts, stars—the six days of creation—
came floating in, gold on a chute of light.
In May, grudging farmers admired the carpet
and foretold a rich year.

                    [Miraculous August! What . . .

Miraculous August! What shelves of yellow capeweed,
what pouffes of everlastings. We worship nature
in my country.

Never such heath as flowered on the virgin slopes
of the terrible armchairs. Never convolvulus
brighter than that which choked the china dogs.
Bushwalkers' Clubs boiled their billies with humility
in chimneys where orchids and treesnakes
luxuriantly intertwined.

A photographer came from *The West Australian*, and ten
teenage reportresses. Teachers of botany
overflowed to the garden.

Indeed, trains were run from Yalgoo and Oodnadatta.
But the neighbours slept behind sealed doors, with feather
dusters beside their beds.

Ruins of the City of Hay

The wind has scattered my city to the sheep.
Capeweed and lovely lupins choke the street
where the wind wanders in great gaunt chimneys of hay
and straws cry out like keyholes.

Our yellow Petra of the fields: alas!
I walk the ruins of forum and capitol,
through quiet squares, by the temples of tranquillity.
Wisps of the metropolis brush my hair.
I become invisible in tears.

This was no ratbags' Eden: these were true haystacks.
Golden, but functional, our mansions sprang from dreams
of architects in love (*O my meadow queen!*)
No need for fires to be lit on the yellow hearthstones;
our walls were warmer than flesh, more sure than igloos.
On winter nights we squatted naked as Esquimaux,
chanting our sagas of innocent chauvinism.

In the street no vehicle passed. No telephone,
doorbell or till was heard in the canyons of hay.
No stir, no sound, but the sickle and the loom,.
and the comments of emus begging by kitchen doors
in the moonlike silence of morning.

Though the neighbour states (said Lao Tse) lie in sight of the
    city
and their cocks wake and their watchdogs warn the
    inhabitants
the men of the city of hay will never go there
all the days of their lives.

But the wind of the world descended on lovely Petra
and the spires of the towers and the statues and belfries fell.
The bones of my brothers broke in the breaking columns.
The bones of my sisters, clasping their broken children,
cracked on the hearthstones, under the rooftrees of hay.
I alone mourn in the temples, by broken altars
bowered in black nightshade and mauve salvation-jane.

And the cocks of the neighbour nations scratch in the straw.
And their dogs rejoice in the bones of all my brethren.

Eskimo Occasion

I am in my Eskimo-hunting-song mood,
Aha!
The lawn is tundra   the car will not start
the sunlight is an avalanche   we are avalanche-struck at our
    breakfast
struck with sunlight through glass   me and my spoonfed
    daughters
out of this world in our kitchen.

I will sing the song of my daughter-hunting,
Oho!
The waves lay down   the ice grew strong
I sang the song   of dark water under ice
the song of winter fishing   the magic for seal rising
among the ancestor-masks.

I waited by water to dream new spirits,
Hoo!
The water spoke   the ice shouted
the sea opened   the sun made young shadows
they breathed my breathing   I took them from deep water
I brought them fur-warmed home.

I am dancing the years of the two great hunts,
Ya-hay!
It was I who waited   cold in the wind-break
I stamp like the bear   I call like the wind of the thaw
I leap like the sea spring-running.   My sunstruck daughters
    splutter
and chuckle and bang their spoons:

Mummy is singing at breakfast and dancing!
So big!

JUDITH RODRIGUEZ

Water a Thousand Feet Deep

I stand washing up, the others have gone out walking.
Being at the best, I am homing in on the worst:

to choke in indifferent waves, over ears in ocean —
skim of earth's sweat—what immensities of salt fear
drench us and tighten—with children to save or lose,
the choice, as from old gods, which to consign to destruction:
how to riddle out waste and defiance? what line cast?
what crying hope hold to? for there is no deciding,
it acts itself, the damning sequence secret
as origin and universe, life as an improvisation
on terrors . . .

the tearaway undertow. But I never lose grasp on my son
or stop swilling plates and setting them to drain;

till blatantly the door. The boy ran ahead of the rest
and is home. I let him in panting, he trails me insisting
Hey, Mum, so close, there is so much floating known here
between us, have we trod the same waters? Hey, Mum,
is there water a thousand feet deep? Yes, I say,
emptying the sink, and give him figures, the soundings
of ocean trenches, which are after all within measure.
As if in the context of fathoms he'd made a mistake
and it mattered.

LES A. MURRAY

A New England Farm, August 1914

August is the windy month,
The month of mares' tails high in heaven,
August is the fiery month,
The windswept doorstep of the year.

But who is this rider on the road
With urgent spurs of burning silver?

August is the winter's death,
He dries the rotted June rain in the earth,
Stiffens fat roots, ignites within the peach tree
Flower and seed. August is time to think
Of facing ploughshares, getting our new boots,
And of the first calves shivering in the grass
Still wet with birth-slime.

But who is this rider at the gate?
Why do the people run to listen?

August is the new year's hinge:
Time out of mind we've stacked the raddled autumn
Cornstalks on the river bank for burning,
Watching the birds come dodging through the smoke
To feast on beetles. Time out of mind
We've retraced last year's furrows with the plough:
How can this August fail us?

Why do the young men saddle horses?
Why do the women grieve together?

LES A. MURRAY

An Absolutely Ordinary Rainbow

The word goes round Repins, the murmur goes round
    Lorenzinis,
At Tattersalls, men look up from sheets of numbers,
The Stock Exchange scribblers forget the chalk in their hands
And men with bread in their pockets leave the Greek Club:
There's a fellow crying in Martin Place. They can't stop him.

The traffic in George Street is banked up for half a mile
And drained of motion. The crowds are edgy with talk
And more crowds come hurrying. Many run in the back streets
Which minutes ago were busy main streets, pointing:
There's a fellow weeping down there. No one can stop him.

The man we surround, the man no one approaches
Simply weeps, and does not cover it, weeps
Not like a child, not like the wind, like a man
And does not declaim it, nor beat his breast, nor even
Sob very loudly—yet the dignity of his weeping

Holds us back from his space, the hollow he makes about him
In the midday light, in his pentagram of sorrow,
And uniforms back in the crowd who tried to seize him
Stare out at him, and feel, with amazement, their minds
Longing for tears as children for a rainbow.

Some will say, in the years to come, a halo
Or force stood around him. There is no such thing.
Some will say they were shocked and would have stopped him
But they will not have been there. The fiercest manhood,
The toughest reserve, the slickest wit amongst us

                    [Trembles with silence, and . . .

Trembles with silence, and burns with unexpected
Judgements of peace. Some in the concourse scream
Who thought themselves happy. Only the smallest children
And such as look out of Paradise come near him
And sit at his feet, with dogs and dusty pigeons.

Ridiculous, says a man near me, and stops
His mouth with his hands, as if it uttered vomit—
And I see a woman, shining, stretch her hand
And shake as she receives the gift of weeping;
As many as follow her also receive it

And many weep for sheer acceptance, and more
Refuse to weep for fear of all acceptance,
But the weeping man, like the earth, requires nothing,
The man who weeps ignores us, and cries out
Of his writhen face and ordinary body

Not words, but grief, not messages, but sorrow
Hard as the earth, sheer, present as the sea—
And when he stops, he simply walks between us
Mopping his face with the dignity of one
Man who has wept, and now has finished weeping.

Evading believers, he hurries off down Pitt Street.

Senryu

Just two hours after
Eternal Life pills came out
Someone took thirty.

LES A. MURRAY

The Ballad of Jimmy Governor

H.M. PRISON, DARLINGHURST, 18TH JANUARY 1901

You can send for my breakfast now, Governor.
The colt from Black Velvet's awake
And the ladies all down from the country
Are gathered outside for my sake.

Soon be all finished, the running.
No tracks of mine lead out here.
Today, I take that big step
On the bottom rung of the air
And be in Heaven for dinner.
Might be the first jimbera there.

The Old People don't go to Heaven,
Good thing. My mother might meet
That stockman feller my father
And him cut her dead in the street.
Mother, today I'll be dancing
Your way and his way on numb feet.

But a man's not a rag to wipe snot on,
I got that much into their heads,
Them hard white sunbonnet ladies
That turned up their short lips and said
My wife had a slut's eye for colour.
I got that into their head

And the cow-cockies' kids plant up chimneys
They got horse soldiers out with the Law
After Joe and lame Jack and tan Jimmy—
But who learnt us how to make war
On women, old men, babies?
It ain't all one way any more.

[The papers, they . . .

Jimbera: half-caste Aboriginal

LES A. MURRAY

The papers, they call us bushrangers:
That would be our style, I daresay,
Bushrangers on foot with our axes.
It sweetens the truth, anyway.
They don't like us killing their women.
Their women kill us every day.

And the squatters are peeing their moleskins,
That's more than a calf in the wheat,
It's Jimmy the fencer, running
Along the top rail in the night,
It's the Breelong mob crossing the ranges
With rabbitskins soft on their feet.

*

But now Jack in his Empire brickyard
Has already give back his shoes
And entered the cleanliness kingdom,
The Commonwealth drums through the walls
And I'm weary of news.

I'm sorry, old Jack, I discharged you
You might have enjoyed running free
Of plonk and wet cornbags and colour
With us pair of outlaws. But see,
You can't trust even half a whitefeller.
You died of White Lady through me.

They tried me once running, once standing:
One time ought to do for the drop.
It's more trial than you got, I hear, Joe,
Your tommyhawk's chipped her last chop.
I hope you don't mind I got lazy
When the leaks in my back made me stop.

White Lady: methylated spirits and powdered milk. A fringe cocktail,
definitely, but not yet obsolete.

If any gin stands in my print
I'll give her womb sorrow and dread,
If a buck finds our shape in the tussocks
I'll whiten the hair in his head,
But a man's not a rag to wipe boots on
And I got that wrote up, bright red,

Where even fine ladies can read it
Who never look at the ground
For a man that ain't fit to breed from
May make a terrible bound
Before the knacker's knife gets him.
Good night to you, father. Sleep sound.

Fetch in my breakfast, Governor,
I have my journey to make
And the ladies all down from the country
Are howling outside for my sake.

The Buladelah–Taree Holiday Song Cycle

1
The people are eating dinner in that country north of Legge's
    Lake;
behind flywire and venetians, in the dimmed cool, town
    people eat Lunch.
Plying knives and forks with a peek-in sound, with a tuck-in
    sound
they are thinking about relatives and inventory, they are
    talking about customers and visitors.
In the country of memorial iron, on the creek-facing hills
    there,
they are thinking about bean plants, and rings of tank water,
    of growing a pumpkin by Christmas;

                              [rolling a cigarette, they . . .

rolling a cigarette, they say thoughtfully Yes, and their
  companion nods, considering.
Fresh sheets have been spread and tucked tight, childhood
  rooms have been seen to,
for this is the season when children return with their children
to the place of Bingham's Ghost, of the Old Timber Wharf, of
  the Big Flood That Time,
the country of the rationalized farms, of the day-and-night
  farms, and of the Pitt Street farms,
of the Shire Engineer and many other rumours, of the tractor
  crankcase furred with chaff,
the places of sitting down near ferns, the snake-fear places, the
  cattle-crossing-long-ago places.

2

It is the season of the Long Narrow City; it has crossed the
  Myall, it has entered the North Coast,
that big stunning snake; it is looped through the hills, burning
  all night there.
Hitching and flying on the downgrades, processionally
  balancing on the climbs,
it echoes in O'Sullivan's Gap, in the tight coats of the flooded-
  gum trees;
the tops of palms exclaim at it unmoved, there near Wootton.
Glowing all night behind the hills, with a north-shifting glare,
  burning behind the hills;
through Coolongolook, through Wang Wauk, across the
  Wallamba,
the booming tarred pipe of the holiday slows and spurts again;
  Nabiac chokes in glassy wind,
the forests on Kiwarric dwindle in cheap light; Tuncurry and
  Forster swell like cooking oil.
The waiting is buffed, in timber villages off the highway, the
  waiting is buffeted:
the fumes of fun hanging above ferns; crime flashes in strange
  windscreens, in the time of the Holiday.
Parasites weave quickly through the long gut that paddocks
  shine into;
powerful makes surging and pouncing: the police, collecting
  Revenue.

The heavy gut winds over the Manning, filling northward,
   digesting the towns, feeding the towns;
they all become the narrow city, they join it;
girls walking close to murder discard, with excitement, their
   names.
Crossing Australia of the sports, the narrow city, bringing
   home the children.

3

It is good to come out after driving and walk on bare grass;
walking out, looking all around, relearning that country.
Looking out for snakes, and looking out for rabbits as well;
going into the shade of myrtles to try their cupped climate,
   swinging by one hand around them,
in that country of the Holiday . . .
stepping behind trees to the dam, as if you had a gun,
to that place of the Wood Duck,
to that place of the Wood Duck's Nest,
proving you can still do it; looking at the duck who hasn't seen
   you,
the mother duck who'd run Catch Me (broken wing) I'm
   Fatter (broken wing), having hissed to her children.

4

The birds saw us wandering along.
Rosellas swept up crying out *we think we think*; they settled
   farther along;
knapping seeds off the grass, under dead trees where their eggs
   were, walking around on their fingers,
flying on into the grass.
The heron lifted up his head and elbows; the magpie stepped
   aside a bit,
angling his chopsticks into pasture, turning things over in his
   head.
At the place of the Plough Handles, of the Apple Trees
   Bending Over, and of the Cattlecamp,
there the vealers are feeding; they are loosely at work, facing
   everywhere.
They are always out there, and the forest is always on the hills;

                 [around the sun are turning . . .

around the sun are turning the wedgetail eagle and her mate,
  that dour brushhook-faced family:
they settled on Deer's Hill away back when the sky was
  opened,
in the bull-oak trees way up there, the place of fur tufted in the
  grass, the place of bone-turds.

5
The Fathers and the Great-Grandfathers, they are out in the
  paddocks all the time, they live out there,
at the place of the Rail Fence, of the Furrows Under Grass, at
  the place of the Slab Chimney.
We tell them that clearing is complete, an outdated attitude,
  all over;
we preach without a sacrifice, and are ignored; flowering
  bushes grow dull to our eyes.
We begin to go up on the ridge, talking together, looking at
  the kino-coloured ants,
at the yard-wide sore of their nest, that kibbled peak, and the
  workers heaving vast stalks up there,
the brisk compact workers; jointed soldiers pour out then,
  tense with acid; several probe the mouth of a lost gin bottle:
Innuendo, we exclaim, *literal minds!* and go on up the ridge,
  announced by finches;
passing the place of the Dingo Trap, and that farm hand it
  caught, and the place of the Cowbails,
we come to the road and watch heifers,
little unjoined devons, their teats hidden in fur, and the cousin
  with his loose-slung stockwhip driving them.
We talk with him about rivers and the lakes; his polished horse
  is stepping nervously,
printing neat omegas in the gravel, flexing its skin to shake off
  flies;
his big sidestepping horse that has kept its stones; it recedes
  gradually, bearing him;
we murmur *stone-horse* and *devilry* to the grinners under grass.

6

Barbecue smoke is rising at Legge's Camp; it is steaming into
the midday air,
all around the lake shore, at the Broadwater, it is going up
among the paperbark trees,
a heat-shimmer of sauces, rising from tripods and flat steel, at
that place of the Cone-shells,
at that place of the Seagrass, and the tiny segmented things
swarming in it, and of the Pelican.
Dogs are running around disjointedly; water escapes from
their mouths,
confused emotions from their eyes; humans snarl at them
Gwanout and Hereboy, not varying their tone much;
the impoverished dog people, suddenly sitting down to nuzzle
themselves; toddlers side with them:
toddlers, running away purposefully at random, among cars,
into big drownie-water (come back, Cheryl-Ann!).
They rise up as charioteers, leaning back on the tow-bar; all
their attributes bulge at once;
swapping swash shoulder-wings for the white-sheeted shoes
that bear them,
they are skidding over the flat glitter, stiff with grace, for once
not travelling to arrive.
From the high dunes over there, the rough blue distance, at
length they come back behind the boats,
and behind the boats' noise, cartwheeling, or sitting down,
into the lake's warm chair;
they wade ashore and eat with the families, putting off that
uprightness, that assertion,
eating with the families who love equipment, and the freedom
from equipment,
with the fathers who love driving, and lighting a fire between
stones.

7

Shapes of children were moving in the standing corn, in the
child-labour districts;
coloured flashes of children, between the green and parching
stalks, appearing and disappearing.
Some places, they are working, racking off each cob like a
lever, tossing it on the heaps;

[other places, they are . . .

other places, they are children of child-age, there playing
    jungle:
in the tiger-striped shade, they are firing hoehandle machine
    guns, taking cover behind fat pumpkins;
in other cases, it is Sunday and they are lovers.
They rise and walk together in the sibilance, finding single
    rows irksome, hating speech now,
or, full of speech, they swap files and follow defiles,
    disappearing and appearing;
near the rain-grey barns, and the children building cattleyards
    beside them;
the standing corn, gnawed by pouched and rodent mice;
    generations are moving among it,
the parrot-hacked, medicine-tasseled corn, ascending all the
    creek flats, the wire-fenced alluvials,
going up in patches through the hills, towards the Steep Country.

8
Forests and State Forests, all down off the steeper country;
    mosquitoes are always living in there:
they float about like dust motes and sink down, at the places of
    the Stinging Tree,
and of the Staghorn Fern; the males feed on plant-stem fluid,
    absorbing that watery ichor;
the females meter the air, feeling for the warm-blooded smell,
    needing blood for their eggs.
They find the dingo in his sleeping-place, they find his
    underbelly and his anus;
they find the possum's face, they drift up the ponderous pleats
    of the fig tree, way up into its rigging,
the high camp of the fruit bats; they feed on the membranes
    and ears of bats; tired wings cuff air at them;
their eggs burning inside them, they alight on the muzzles of
    cattle,
the half-wild bush cattle, there at the place of the Sleeper
    Dump, at the place of the Tallowwoods.
The males move about among growth tips; ingesting solutions,
    they crouch intently;
the females sing, needing blood to breed their young, their
    singing is in the scrub country;
their tune comes to the name-bearing humans, who dance to it
    and irritably grin at it.

9

The warriors are cutting timber with brash chainsaws; they
  are trimming hardwood pit-props and loading them;
Is that an order? they hoot at the peremptory lorry driver, who
  laughs; he is also a warrior.
They are driving long-nosed tractors, slashing pasture in the
  dinnertime sun;
they are fitting tappets and valves, the warriors, or giving
  finish to a surfboard.
Addressed on the beach by a pale man, they watch waves
  break and are reserved, refusing pleasantry;
they joke only with fellow warriors, chaffing about try-ons and
  the police, not slighting women.
Making Timber a word of power, Con-rod a word of power,
  Sense a word of power, the Regs, a word of power,
they know belt-fed from spring-fed; they speak of being *stiff,*
  and being *history*;
the warriors who have killed, and the warriors who eschewed
  killing,
the solemn, the drily spoken, the life peerage of endurance;
  drinking water from a tap,
they watch boys who think hard work a test, and boys who
  think it is not a test.

10

Now the ibis are flying in, hovering down on the wetlands,
on those swampy paddocks around Darawank, curving down
  in ragged dozens,
on the riverside flats along the Wang Wauk, on the
  Boolambayte pasture flats,
and away towards the sea, on the sand moors, at the place of
  the Jabiru Crane,
leaning out of their wings, they step down; they take out their
  implement at once,
out of its straw wrapping, and start work; they dab
  grasshopper and ground-cricket
with nonexistence . . . spiking the ground and puncturing it . . .
  they swallow down the outcry of a frog;
they discover titbits kept for them under cowmanure lids,
  small slow things.

                    [Pronging the earth, they . . .

Pronging the earth, they make little socket noises, their
    thoughtfulness jolting down-and-up suddenly;
there at Bunyah, along Firefly Creek, and up through
    Germany,
the ibis are all at work again, thin-necked ageing men towards
    evening; they are solemnly all back
at Minimbah, and on the Manning, in the rye-and-clover
    irrigation fields;
city storemen and accounts clerks point them out to their
    wives,
remembering things about themselves, and about the ibis.

11

Abandoned fruit trees, moss-tufted, spotted with dim lichen
    paints; the fruit trees of the Grandmothers,
they stand along the creekbanks, in the old home paddocks,
    where the houses were;
they are reached through bramble-grown front gates, they
    creak at dawn behind burnt skillions,
at Belbora, at Bucca Wauka, away in at Burrell Creek,
at Telararee of the gold-sluices.
The trees are split and rotten-elbowed; they bear the old-
    fashioned summer fruits,
the annual bygones: china pear, quince, persimmon;
the fruit has the taste of former lives, of sawdust and parlour
    song, the tang of Manners;
children bite it, recklessly,
at what will become for them the place of the Slab Wall, and
    of the Coal Oil Lamp,
the place of moss-grit and swallows' nests, the place of the
    Crockery.

12

Now the sun is an applegreen blindness through the swells, a
    white blast on the sea-face, flaking and shoaling;
now it is burning off the mist, it is emptying the density of
    trees, it is spreading upriver,
hovering above the casuarina needles, there at Old Bar and
    Manning Point;
flooding the island farms, it abolishes the milkers' munching
    breath

as they walk towards the cowyards; it stings a bucket here, a
    teatcup there.
Morning steps into the world by ever more southerly gates;
    shadows weaken their north skew
on Middle Brother, on Cape Hawke, on the dune scrub
    toward Seal Rocks;
steadily the heat is coming on, the butter-water time, the
    clothes-sticking time;
grass covers itself with straw; abandoned things are thronged
    with spirits;
everywhere wood is still with strain; birds hiding down the
    creek galleries, and in the cockspur canes;
the cicada is hanging up her sheets; she takes wing off her
    music-sheets.
Cars pass with a rational zoom, panning quickly towards
    Wingham,
through the thronged and glittering, the shale-topped ridges,
    and the cattlecamps,
towards Wingham for the cricket, the ball knocked hard in
    front of smoked-glass ranges, and for the drinking.
In the time of heat, the time of flies around the mouth, the
    time of the west veranda,
looking at that umbrage along the ranges, on the New
    England side;
clouds begin assembling vaguely, a hot soiled heaviness on the
    sky, away there towards Gloucester;
a swelling up of clouds, growing there above Mount George,
    and above Tipperary;
far away and hot with light; sometimes a storm takes root
    there, and fills the heavens rapidly;
darkening, boiling up and swaying on its stalks, pulling this
    way and that, blowing round by Krambach;
coming white on Bulby, it drenches down on the paddocks,
    and on the wire fences;
the paddocks are full of ghosts, and people in cornbag hoods
    approaching;
lights are lit in the house; the storm veers mightily on its stem,
    above the roof; the hills uphold it;

                    [the stony hills guide . . .

the stony hills guide its dissolution; gullies opening and
     crumbling down, wrenching tussocks and rolling them;
the storm carries a greenish-grey bag; perhaps it will find hail
     and send it down, starring cars, flattening tomatoes,
in the time of the Washaways, of the dead trunks braiding
     water, and of the Hailstone Yarns.

13
The stars of the holiday step out all over the sky.
People look up at them, out of their caravan doors and their
     campsites;
people look up from the farms, before going back; they gaze at
     their year's worth of stars.
The Cross hangs head-downward, out there over Markwell;
it turns upon the Still Place, the pivot of the Seasons, with one
     shoulder rising:
'Now I'm beginning to rise, with my Pointers and my
     Load . . .'
hanging eastwards, it shines on the sawmills and the lakes, on
     the glasses of the Old People.
Looking at the Cross, the galaxy is over our left shoulder, slung
     up highest in the east;
there the Dog is following the Hunter; the Dog Star pulsing
     there above Forster; it shines down on the Bikies,
and on the boat-hire sheds, there at the place of the Oyster;
     the place of the Shark's Eggs and her Hide;
the Pleiades are pinned up high on the darkness, away back
     above the Manning;
they are shining on the Two Blackbutt Trees, on the rotted
     river wharves, and on the towns;
standing there, above the water and the lucerne flats, at the
     place of the Families;
their light sprinkles down on Taree of the Lebanese shops, it
     mingles with the streetlights and their glare.
People recover the starlight, hitching north,
travelling north beyond the seasons, into that country of the
     Communes, and of the Banana:
the Flying Horse, the Rescued Girl, and the Bull, burning
     steadily above that country.
Now the New Moon is low down in the west, that remote
     direction of the Cattlemen,

LES A. MURRAY

and of the Saleyards, the place of steep clouds, and of the
    Rodeo;
the New Moon who has poured out her rain, the moon of the
    Planting-times.
People go outside and look at the stars, and at the melon-rind
    moon,
the Scorpion going down into the mountains, over there
    towards Waukivory, sinking into the tree-line,
in the time of the Rockmelons, and of the Holiday . . .
the Cross is rising on his elbow, above the glow of the horizon;
carrying a small star in his pocket, he reclines there brilliantly,
above the Alum Mountain, and the lakes threaded on the
    Myall River, and above the Holiday.

PETER STEELE

Living/Dying

for Barney Carroll

There may be a moment, just before the face
    collapses into a vizard, and men
begin to attend where they can no longer aid,
    when eyes are seen for their own sake.
The one in his passion does not have a future,
    but the eyes are still created by
what they regard: and those who dare to look
    are haled back from all their evasions
to the candle of the body. Shock and fever
    are coursing now with larger claims
than his poisoned blood can make, the filaments
    of flesh are marbling, minute by minute,

                                    [he is turning . . .

he is turning into his past; but now as then
    he lives as he dies, of his whole life,
glowing towards his own darkness. The doctor
    moves as he does, each uncertain
which of the two is Dante, which a Virgil
    familiar of the descent. There are words
for each to use, the rituals of affection,
    so long as they have time and spittle:
there is gear to coil and fix, as if this voyage
    led back to harbour from around
some other world: and there are those who stand
    like ornaments for a razed temple,
as impotent as stone. When it all changes
    in the usual way, when the doctor makes
the first move and the last, his eyes too
    are things to see and be believed.
Watching it happen, he can see the world
    as a frail ball in space, mottled
with cloud and broken coastline, shifting around
    its own unsteady centre. The lawn
outside the window might be a mirage,
    those men and women figurines
of interstellar dust. Dying alone
    may be our fashion, but we take
the light from many eyes for company;
    and this man, our first recourse,
the last witness of our carnal presence,
    is plundered more than most. Thank God
there is something else for him to see, as daily
    the blind, new-born eyes promise
fidelity to life. There will be teachers
    to match as best they can the ripeness,
which is nearly all, with this uncovenanted
    yearning to become, already,
two have paid tribute, out of pain and pleasure,
    for a life received but never earned:
but here, standing between the ones who tender
    and the ones who name and question, is
someone to signify. He must labour,
    his mind in his hands, at bone and muscle,

must thumb volumes like some deserted scholar,
    must wake in his exhaustion. Still,
what he is tending, pious or technical,
    is a life that moves by naked hope.
Explorers may conquer: the Stone Age surgeon bent
    over a skull trephined by flint
would keep the fragments for an amulet,
    and fend off demons through assay;
when Leonardo, tired and tireless, worked
    with probe for pencil, bodies rose
from piteous clay to Adam, a child to be
    furled awake in the womb, and the last
hostage of a violent season quickened,
    alight at least on the page. Those men,
anonymous or heroic, propagate
    a love of the flesh as part of the world's
body, the being no less holy in
    its sickness than in what is called
its health. And if, beset by all the terrors
    they try to abate with names chosen
from a dead language, they falter in their way—
    blind to a lethal tumour, deaf
to what is behind an auscultation, numb
    to things piercing another heart—
let us have mercy on the harried few
    who try to have mercy on us. True,
we minister to them, as we lie before them,
    figures of their mortality,
bringing to birth a life we bear together;
    but as one does not love a place
the less for having suffered long in its confines,
    one may be healed through a last compassion.

GEOFFREY LEHMANN

Out after Dark

I'm only sorry I've no child to show him.
Out driving after dusk my headlights fumble
Through dust and trees, undulate over tarred roads.
My father somewhere in the night is plodding
Dark hills he cannot understand, loose earth,
My father innocent, frail as rice paper,
Mild at the end, not knowing he has cancer,
But knowing that he's finished, gentle, silent,
So selling bit by bit his watches, silver,
The crumbling mansion with its vast verandas,
Its palms and cedar doors with cut-glass handles
Hiving the light in honey-coloured facets,
House where we never lived, our lives unlived.
My headlights brush moths, scrub, and scan and wander,
But what I'm looking for is past not present,
A hot night twenty years ago, myself
A child reading *The Moonstone*, all of us waiting
In canvas chairs for trains eternally late,
Bells ringing as we lumber luggage aboard,
Pineapple fields lit by our passing carriage.
Reflected in the glass, our figures seated
Beneath a lamp travel dark fields and rivers.
Loving, transitory, we never existed.

The Telescope at Siding Springs

The Warrumbungles loomed like derelict whales.
All night the whispering bush, dark, empty landscape
Gaunt mountains under shoals of browsing stars
Condensed their thoughts as lonely country does.
In woollen earmuffs, jackets firmly zipped
They moved in windless cold, boots sharp on concrete,
And the great mirror slowly turning followed
And drank a scratch of light their eyes were blind to.
Patiently magnified for hours through mirrors
A star chiselled a message on dark film,
A tentative diamond flickered in frail water.

ANDREW TAYLOR

The Nocturne in the Corner Phonebox

Someone is playing a trombone
in the telephone box outside my room.
It's 1 a.m.,
and he's removed the globe.
He's playing a melancholy cadenza
probably over the S.T.D.
to his girl in Sydney.

I can imagine . . .
she's curled to the telephone
listening to that impossible music
a smile curving her face.
I wonder if he has enough change
for all those extensions.
Could he reverse the charge?

Somebody called Hugh Adamson
blares out a nocturne in a phone box.
His father's old and dying,
his mother's dead, his girl's away,
he's very sad, his nocturne's very sad,
his trombone blares and flares and says
'He's very sad, yair yair, he's very sad'.

Maybe he's only playing to a friend
in East St Kilda.
Maybe he hasn't any change.
Someone is playing a trombone—impossible—
in the phone box with the door shut.
I've no idea who he is. I'm waiting
for my phone to ring. I like this music.

ANDREW TAYLOR

Cosimo

R.I.P. ROME 1964

When he died I threw him over the wall
he lay like a length of sash cord
till the ants

to put a python in a rubbish bin
I couldn't

next door the American School
shaded by pines and oleanders
he'd died in a suitcase
he needed grass mice most of all grass
flicker of shadow
moving things

his eyes had flicked
digital
and his tongue
I cried when he died

he might have grown twenty feet
so many shoes belts handbags
I'd have sold him to the zoo
he'd have eaten my cat

That was the year I almost bought a lute
I remember looking at snakeskin things with my wife
we didn't buy on Via del Corso

his skeleton was plaited chalk
in the long rushing grass
he'd balanced like a circus on my arm
he'd smuggled through four lots of customs
once

in the Paris metro
he'd charmed a whole carriage of Parisians
fighting his way
out of a bag

ROGER McDONALD

Two Summers in Moravia

That soldier with a machinegun bolted
to his motorcycle, I was going to say
ambled down to the pond to take
what geese he wanted; but he didn't.

This was whole days before the horizon trembled.

In the farmyard all the soldier did
was ask for eggs and milk.
He and the daughter (mother sweeping)
stood silent, the sky rounded
like a blue dish.

This was a day
when little happened,
though inch by inch everything changed.
A load of hay narrowly crossed the bridge,
the boy caught a fish underneath in shade,
and ducks quarrelled in the reeds.
Surrounded by wheat, everyone heard the wind
whisper, at evening, as though grain already threshed
was poured from hand to hand.

This was a day possible to locate, years later,
on a similar occasion; geese alive,
the sky uncracked like a new dish,
even the wheat hissing with rumour.
I was going to say unchanged
completely, but somewhere behind
the soldier had tugged his cap,
kicked the motor to harsh life
and swayed off,
the nose of the machinegun tilted up.

JENNIFER J. RANKIN

Green Ash

Dreaming of that place I wake.
Outside my window pale wistaria
is climbing again in the ageing peach tree
the crack in the ceiling of my room
forms patterns and I stumble once more
over my absent father's shadow in the hall.

Summers spent hiding in the itching kapok vine
reading a book while the others wash up
tough fighting in gangs whose hardware is rocks
lessons in cricket from the red-headed boy
who, neighbours whisper, later majored in Greek.

Long days lying, homesick, from school
listening for the baker's horse
warm bread left on our back verandah table.
My mother in the dining-room is sewing for Christmas.

Years passing jumping off front verandah steps
'statues', falling, freezing in evening light.
Slow months of waiting, watching
the dogs, cats, even the canary,
hoping one day to catch them mating.

Through the last winters the house is brightly lit
burning in the night for children leaving.
Trees curl close about its windows
Red is its long drive winding
Dark is the kapok vine
Cracked are the patterns about me
Slow! I cry out to wistaria strangling the peach tree.

from *The Alphabet Murders*

XI

Karl Marx is a comic novelist, almost—
but when we read *Das Kapital* between the jokes we find
there is a theory of religion, then one of philosophy,
a quick adventure and a sordid tale of justice, and soon
a kind of parable emerges like a shadow on a screen:
man is born, grows up and dies. But if this is all he says
we would be cheated, and the authority of the work
is proof of something more than entertainment.
It is like a factory which, on weekdays,
choked and smoking in a parody of industry
yet holds prospect of a new revival of the workers,
and which on the weekend sinks into a profound silence
that embodies not only the concept of the easy
forty-hour week, but also the executive's retreat
from that which, though stained and horrible,
provides him with a pretty secretary, a young boy,
a lunch account, and fears of bloody revolution.
(Don't cry at the end of that novel, it's ridiculous
unless you cry glycerine which is sly and tricky
and all the kids here will love you for it
you witty bastard and envy your 'attack'
or your nerve and pat you on the back and then
leave you to your own devices. It happens.)
And think of this: each Russian movie masterpiece
bears his stamp, more than an individual approach,
which is like—uh—like a buried emblem
of the work itself, a tiny mirror for the plot—
or maybe narrative—and in this frame
the image, drift and meaning of the total work
act out their small and wistful life.
Outside this interlocking blazon, a life-style
called 'the film' takes place happily
night after night millions of times
as wasteful and expensive as a Russian dictionary
and more misleading than the tracks it leaves
entering and leaving your life,

[and what is . . .

JOHN TRANTER

and what is that? Snow, politics, the cruel city,
that goodly pedagogic food you ate—
all right, I'm moving, through a dense topography
keeping an eye on how the colourful natives
act out a plausible way of seeing it
for our benefit as we hike away,
leaving behind everything we possibly can.
Getting out is easy, but how you get in—
say, back through a locked window
into a room and a dead love affair
you abandoned the night your future called—
blue moonlight, vinyl floor, lots of mice,
and three creeps in bed—that's different,
that's destructive like a zoo brings tears easily,
so take it easy and forget the lot: Karl Marx,
the parasites, the lovers and the zoo
and run out in the beautiful 'life'
that awaits you. Goodbye.

ROBERT ADAMSON

Sonnets to be written from Prison

O to be 'in the news' again—now as fashion runs
everything would go for 'prison sonnets': I'd be on my own.
I could, once more, go out with pale skin
from my veritable dank cell—the sufferer, poking fun
at myself in form, with a slightly twisted tone.
My stance ironic—one-out, on the run.
Though how can I? I'm not locked up: imagine a typewriter
in solitary. I dream my police unable to surrender—
I'm bored with switching roles and playing
with my gender; the ironies seem incidental, growing thin.
Here's the world—maybe what's left of it—
held together by an almost experimental sonnet.
Surely there must be some way out of poetry other than
Mallarmé's: still-life with bars and shitcan.

ROBERT ADAMSON

Once more, almost a joke—this most serious endeavour
is too intense: imagine a solitary typewriter? Somehow
fashion runs its course; and I'm not in pain.
So there's hardly any need to play on abstract repetitions
to satisfy a predecessor, poet or lawbreaker: I won't be clever—
all the clever crims are not inside the prisons.
Here's the world—maybe what's left of my pretences—
I dream of being carried off to court again:
a sufferer, where all my deities would speak in stern
almost sardonic voices. 'Your Honour, please—
bring me to my senses.' There, I love confessions!
Imagine writing prison sonnets four years after my release.
If only all my memories could be made taciturn
by inventing phrases like: imagine the solitary police.

Yes Your Honour, I know this is ridiculous—although—
I'm 'in the news'. I couldn't bring myself to do
one of those *victimless crimes*: I must suffer in more ways
than one. My crime's pretence is not to overthrow
social order, or to protest—it's my plan
to bring poetry and lawbreaking where they interplay:
imagine newspapers in solitary. I'd walk right through
the court taking down copy 'catch me if you can'—
Defendant in contempt. There has to be a fight,
I can't imagine anything when I'm not up against a law.
Now here's the world—our country's first stone institution,
where inmates still abase themselves at night.
If I was in solitary I could dream—a fashionable bore,
writing books on drugs, birds or revolution.

I dreamed I saw the morning editions settle on the court—
emblazoned with my name, my *story* so glib it made
no sense. The judge said 'emotional' but I thought
of the notoriety. This was the outward world, my sad tirade
was 'news'.—Though, if I'd been rhyming sonnets
in solitary, my suffering alone could've made them *art*.
Now, imagine an illiterate in prison—but I've no regrets
I enjoy my lagging, I feel sorry for the warders.

[The discipline always . . .

ROBERT ADAMSON

The discipline always pulls me through, and my counterpart,
the screw, is tougher with the easy boarders.
This experience might feel profound—though irony's never
broken laws—so I'm against everything
but practical intuitions. My 'solitary etc' is too clever
by half now—but again—who's suffering?

I brood in solitary; it's a way to flagellation, thinking
of my 'day of release'—I shuffle friends as dates
on my calendar, marking them off at random.
Here's the world—the stewed tea I'm drinking
cold—O I suffer. When I walk through the front gates
into the country, what will I become?
I'll throw away the sufferer's comforting mask,
and turn against my memories, leaving a trail of perdition
behind me. Children and women will fall to my simple
intuitive reactions—not even the new journalists will ask
questions: nothing will be capable of feeding on
my actions and survive. My prison sonnets will be drugs
relieving pain: I have remembered helpless men
knocking their bars for hours with aluminium mugs—

We will take it seriously as we open our morning paper.
Someone's broken loose, another child's been
wounded by a pen-knife. A small fire down the bottom
of a suburban garden smells of flesh. Dark circles under
the mother's eyes appear on television; she's seen
her baby at the morgue. Our country moves closer to the
    world:
a negro's book is on the shelves. The criminal's become
mythologized; though yesterday he curled
over and didn't make the news. So the myth continues,
    growing
fat and dangerous on a thousand impractical intuitions.
The bodies of old sharks hang on the butcher's hooks.
In broad day somewhere a prisoner is escaping.
The geriatrics are suddenly floating in their institutions.
The myth is torn apart and stashed away in books.

ROBERT ADAMSON

The River

A step is taken, and all the world's before me.
Night so clear,

stars hang in the low branches,
small-fires, riding waves of thin atmosphere,

islands parting tide as meteors burn air.

Oysters powder to chalk in my hands.

A flying fox collides against my trunk
as the first memory unfurls.

Rocks on the shoreline milling the star-fire,
and each extinguished star,

an angel set free from the tide's long drive.

The memory shines—its fragments falling into place,
and the heavens revealing themselves

as my roots trail, deep nets
between channel and shoal, gathering in

cosmic spinel, Milky Way, Gemini.

I look all about; God, I search all around me.

She surrounds me here
as the light transfigures light

the butterfly exploding herself, colours thrown over
the nets of lights in transfiguration.

The sea's adrift, tails outspread, the harbour dawn.
A gale in my hair as mountains move in.

I drift over lake, through surf-break
and valley. Shifting before me

[another . . .

ROBERT ADAMSON

another place. *On the edge or place inverted*
from Ocean starts another place,

before me—entangled of trees, unseemly
in this time, this place.

Humming nerves of the tide, the eels
twine themselves round, loop and flick

glow through valleys of silt, rise breaking surface,
twisting light, dislodging

memory from its original lineaments.

Tonight time is its own universe, shining in mangroves
through opaque leaves, bodies, plumage

and hands across tide.
The old fear returns through the monument of a fishbone,

and wings of an ice bird waving from rockface
with hardly an instinct.

A step back and my love's before me,
life shot through with these savage changes.

The memory ash—we face each other alone now
with no God to answer to.

After centuries, almost together now
the threshold in sight.

We turn in the rushing tide again and again to each other,
making fire of this, and setting it

here between swamp-flower and star.

To let love go forth to the world's end,
to set our lives in the Centre.

Though the tide turns the river back on itself,
and at its mouth, Ocean.

CHRISTINE CHURCHES

Autumn—for My Son

Sunlight there is crisped to stone,
air breaks gently round the walls;
the warmth hives close
and stones become a honeycomb of light,
blocked and shaped against a young blue sky.
The soft-tweed wind billows the trees;
poplar-leaves are shells of light
hanging by threads to the last of summer;
while sparrows hop in the cobbled shadows,
drowse and sink in the homespun warmth.

At night, the soft dusk purple blooms around the walls.
The light is mulled through the window panes;
comes flowing through the loosely skeined trees in a long,
    warm swell.
I cannot see the grass, but the smell is there;
and I think of home . . .

The new-baked freshness of an autumn day;
muscled warmth of horse's flank,
the tail-jerking bleat of strong-grown lambs
as we bring them in for tailing.
I hug their woolly brightness close to my face,
laugh at their twigged and branching cry.

And now it is autumn again,
and this petal-thin cry is the cry of my son,
I hold him close between my arms,
and feel him breathe, and breathe,
and breathe.

GARY CATALANO

A Poem is Not

A young but gloomy man
I'll never understand
that true poetic art
of writing from the heart.

A telegraphic line
is like a skinny vine
unweighed by any fruit.
I don't like poems which bruit

the heart's convulsions, or
put signs above the door
inviting all to peek
at what went on last week.

Poets must do more
than note their fondness for
the human species; if,
demurring, they insist

on passion or the like
and so uncaulk that dyke
no ogre's chilblained eye
shall water when they die.

The art, in poetry,
is not, like therapy,
an existential rub:
a poem is not a pub.

Discovering Parts of a Body

Stepping out of the bath
my left heel from this angle looks very tender,
by which I mean inoffensive,
like an apple,
small, clean, thin-skinned, a nob of sweet Jonathan.

I suddenly consider the consequences
of stepping on jagged glass,
thick glass, a broken soft drink bottle;
my heel crunching down unwarily,
the skin split,
the sharp, hard point lurching up
till something screams inside;
like having my heart bared
and probed with a finger.

A dull strangeness
in looking at things closely;
I'll pretend I'm an Eastern lady
with heels like two ripe fruit.
The Hordes, when they catch me will want
to twist them off,
and eat them slice by slice.

Underneath the House

I

It must have been summer,
the time my sister dared me to come underneath the house.
There was a smell of spiders
in the low dirt corridors
and the dark passed our eyes
like a continuous cat making us blind.

[We moved . . .

We moved on our haunches
breaking cobwebs,
scraping the wall with sticks.
When we heard dulled footsteps
overhead, we held so still I saw our breaths
drift out, looping and falling
losing shape thinly.

In the last room the light
was brown, and the rubble there, once damp for a plant,
now dead as a foot,
dry as an old man's ankle.

II

My father kept his tools under the house;
on a long plank bench were nails and slivers,
boxes and slices of metal
and bits of shattered picture glass and glass-wool padding
to line the gramophone;
over it all the smell of linseed
and the growing spoor of crates of mushrooms.

In bed I would listen to the sounds downstairs
of hammering and planing keeping on into the cool hours.
My father with red cedar
dovetailing corners
staining and polishing in small oily circles
or smoothing an edge, the wood hissing,
shavings curling and dropping to the floor.

III

I dream that I run with no shoes
down a cement path
towards a sound and a square of light.
This night is the cylinder
of a brown glass jar;
Hands on my head I push up for air.

SUSAN WHITING

Sifting Stones at Capri

The striped pebbles somersault
like cats through my fingers.
They are lovely and wet.
There. A pale green one! My son puts it in his mouth.
We are sitting in shallow water,
we are lulled by little waves,
we are watching the stones turn easily in their sleep.
There are white waxy ones, round pieces
of honey-amber, smooth diffuse sapphires,
worn-round chips of azure terracotta tiles,
fragments of vases and houses,
buttons from torn children's clothing.

The waves break into gentle hollowed dapples,
into rainbowed water-pebbles stroking each other.
They batter my legs gently,
the rain of little stones plop into my harbour
—my legs are the shores of a narrow estuary,
fragrant pines cup the cliffs, my mountain legs
grind the stones underneath
into postures of greater intimacy—
waves pummel my skin,
they wear down the flesh,
lap it away like cat tongues lap milk.
When I am worn my arms will unhug my knees,
my bones will lie down and float off
like wrecked cities
under the rock spell of water,
and be rubbed and rubbed into ovals of ivory.

Perhaps a child sifting pebbles
will find them, my quartz and ivory eyes,
and string them, and wear them like eggs
in the hollows of his throat . . .
shells, bells which will sing for him
at low tide, when I begin rising in moonsway.

MICHAEL DRANSFIELD

Courland Penders: Going Home

At the end of the road are stone posts, two either side of
a cattle grid. Trees cripple sight with a bias of green. Beyond
the gates, an elm drive winds among fields
to the house. This is unnoticeable, horizoned by spectacular
    ranges;
enforested, a Vlaminck 'House In the Woods'.
Halfway along the row of twelve-pane windows downstairs,
a heavy door. One opens it with a key rusty from disuse.
The hall is hung with portraits, hunting scenes,
minor Nativities and forgotten Madonnas. Corridor. Enfilade
    through
rooms which gape coldly. Dust sheets smother the furniture,
there is a rustle of mice disappearing.
It is dim even when the shutters have been prised apart, brown
    shadow
unexorcised. The gale outside anthems a dead family. Night
comes down and there is nothing then. Impersonal fire in a
    ghostly hearth.
When morning passes like a train at a level-crossing, who else
    will know?
Draw the curtains there is no world without. No patchwork
    Herefords
grazing; no wife or sons; only a crop of brambles; only rabbits
    to be shot
from a verandah rail. Dream
of a white horse in sunset pasture, or that someone will come.
    Futilities.
The calendar accelerates, days are empty but for lists and
    numbers.
All the corners have spiders, suggesting Dostoevsky's Eternity.
    Permanence
was their material, whose nameless builders, the house
    outlived even the strongest.
It will be a mortuary soon. These poems are stillborn,
    anachronists, insubstantial.
Suicide would be wasted, death comes soon enough.
If one has nowhere further to go, it is not important
how long one takes to get there, or by what means one travels.

ALAN WEARNE

St Bartholomew remembers Jesus Christ as an Athlete

Always in training. Yet helping with his work
was, partly boring, sometimes even nasty.
Still, even when I felt he'd gone too far,
think: here we go again, out came the logic
smooth as a circle, Roman-disciplined.
Brilliant. Yes. Yet never near to God.

Only when he ran.
Only when I saw him striding.
(He'd leap and throw his arms above his head.)
It really was a case of 'run with me'.
I did. And often we came down the mountains,
(jogging loosely—never with a cramp).
My running partner—heading for Jerusalem—
appeared as if his feet were next to God.

This too was a feat,—running for a month,
(as rumour had it).
        Sprinting in the temple
was nothing less than perfect. Tables knocked,
Whips raised and money lost,
He charged them twice.

Of course revenge was needed, and his arms
were raised once more; his feet, however, broken;
sort of enforced retirement. Still,
he made a comeback, to end all comebacks:
                     Once
there were ten, and I half-walking, pacing,
(my room mates seated, limbered-up in thought).
We stopped the noise and movement; standing still
I heard the footsteps pounding up the stairs.

ALAN WEARNE

Eating Out

for Robin Rattray-Wood

Gentle, inaffluent,
susceptible to portions of pity though
a mild cynicism increased
as he left high school and
The High School Students Union:
articulates in berets with
little yellow stars, 'semantics man,'
'aww that's a cop-out, man!'
Susceptible to cool correct sympathy
(slight commitment,)
any girl concerned to teach him
wines driving; boredom.

And Nicol, she was joining NIDA yet
they kept company for few weeks
of a dry summer, (shifts and
blouses flapping over the line.)
What's she like to live with?
Ahh that's romance, attainable
as clap. All construction:
a partner in sorrow would be
wonderful: poor pet, poor pet. (Such
prey we are to prey!)

Windows of dwarfs, in Xmas
the city was presentiments, expenditure,
recalled for him an earlier attempt
—each day begins a year—
'how often should I see you?'
the mother with hands smeared
in dry-cleaning fluid. Nice
nice nice nice. He shivered
for their kingdom of constraint,
but no quibbles, virginity is
amazing, beautiful as the back
of Sarah's waist.
How neat it was!

'See a show?' 'You're hosting!' Then
lets. Mrs Salmons (was it Salmons?) suspected
at least, casinos. 'Where will tea
be?' Hinting at liquor. 'Eh?'
Why it's toast, Ma'm, it's an evangelical
coffee house, Ma'm. Shook hands.
Coming back her father beaming: Young Ones,
and Sarah asked excuse me,
left for sleep. That body,
small neat redoubtable, it
seemed unfair; but quit the thought.
We were a debacle!

This year, Nicol. On weekends,
before her course,
they trotted round the palm-tree parks,
up to rotundas, her home at hand,
through lime-white colonnades, there,
a lot for him:
table manners, the correct liquor. Some
minor heiress in a cheesecloth blouse
sustaining his dictum:
'My Word, Marxism is exotic!'

[For last year . . .

For last year (as a friend referred,)
Les Chinois, stoic in Bakeries, their cache
of humourless invective; yet, o the design!

Living is divergence, plus
'how swell'. A trainee life-assessor and
Sarah would be very very happy. Not hers
some fuming dialectician;
their High School Students Union pronounced
such ministry: 'Lethal as a nail gun.'
Some years further,
here's he, sitting in a bandstand, the
NIDA trainee saying, 'sometimes
I can't conceive of letting a man near,
you understand?' Romance is, you know,
danger, though a few nights
before her parents drove Nicki
over to the flight, she took him
eating. 'Dad's a solicitor
with conscience.' Workingmen mean
a lot, and the waiter asked him, *him,*
regards wine, 'Sir?'

Damn brief, ought to have been
forgettable, (I'm forgettable too,) kissing
this forthcoming actress, oh poised for
an unsorrowing wave off the tarmac—
the outsized sunglasses, the smart
pudding-basin bum, cheesecloth.

A lift? Please.
On his prize bush, aphis, Nicol's father
stated, aphis and how to end it,
(talking of steps to Mr Potter, gardener.)
Yes, a lift . . . *with music to town*
and you in my arms . . . easy, adult, radio
smarmed away its happy day happy day.

ROBERT HARRIS

Tobacco

Flavour the days, tobacco.
Bind together a cluster of months
With the other aromas of places
Where they're spent. Become the clean
White odour of the woodchips, place
Of the melting ice cream on the street
And parting veil through which an eye
Alters a life as its prisms shift;

One more branch line out to the upcountry
Where fossickers have to find rivers fit
To squat beside, to endlessly sift.
What will it be?

It will be light and dark ready rubbed
In a gaudy box,
Shared with the mud on a hop farm at planting time.
Rice papers tearing your lips, the stale
Tobacco no more than a nominal pause
In what later will come to be felt as years
Of grinding, repetitive, ceaseless noise.

It will be in the morning,
That first one had on the way to work
Among the dumb files
That are forever hinting
Something about the facts they record
Which slips from sheet to shuffled sheet
Evasively, a grey
Taste to match the midwinter.

[And it will be . . .

And it will be fine to sit at noon
On a broken drum in the loading bay
Smoking and nodding the universe by
For fully half an hour in the sun.

Thin housewives will light up another one
In the chain securing hope and harangue,
The lubricating cups of tarry tea . . .

Immaculate cooks will step outside
For a smoke. Step briefly away
From the kitchen routine
They could follow by rote wearing blindfold.
They will reflect
On the boring adventure that does not admit
The slowly hunting, ever following
Processes of the dark. Maybe they'll note
The cheery tree's thousand new blossoms
Heaved about on an august wind
Fly and return like tethered snow.

It will be whatever the penniless hands
Can lay a hold on, whatever butts
Come wallowing by
On the water hands hold that have to reach
Out to each slim possibility.
Hands that would upend the sky!

And present, too, at a junction of roads,
Thick and silent when only taxis cruise
Across and across the overpass like sharks
And each choice leads only to one avenue—

ROBERT HARRIS

The curdling smoke recreates and revolves
The scene below it absently, abandons direction
Becoming a daybreak of hair
Strewn on a pillow, a flock of wings
Beating above an imagined bay—
Gull's wings, a gull's beak
Opened to large blue areas in a cry.
Then steadies, gathers, exactly rolls
The pillow's curve and the beat of blood
The tiger springing along the nerve.

Made for ignition and burning
What will it be? The packets of days
Curling up in long fingers to rest on a shelf in the air

That are left there
To dissolve

JOHN FORBES

Ode to Tropical Skiing

for Mandy Connell

After breakfast in the Philippines
I take a bath
                  & it's a total fucking gas

Enjoy that ice cream, Gerald,
                  the sun sparkling
                  on its white frostiness
is the closest you'll ever get to St Moritz,
racing up the tiny snow fields on the side of a pill
                  as beside you the young girl's
mirrored goggles reflect all Switzerland
like a chocolate box at the speed of sound
                  & like the ashtray he/she you & it
                  are a total fucking gas

[Asleep in . . .

Asleep in
the milk bars
daylight saving annuls our tuxedo
                 & happy to breathe again
like a revived dance craze
we gulp fresh air, our speeches to the telephone
         so various,
                   so beautiful—
           who loves at close range
           like they do thru a tube?
& when the sun polishes the wires gold then invisible
           a million cheer-up telegrams
           collapse in the snow
while Mandy & I have a glass of Coca-Cola
           as we fly past the moon &
after the piano goes to sleep in our arms
                we wake up
                & it's a total fucking gas

                Was that a baby
or a shirt factory?
no one can tell in this weather, for tho
the tropics are slowly drifting apart & a
           vicious sludge blurs
           the green banks of the river, a chalet
drifts thru the novella where I compare thee
           to a surfboard lost in Peru,
           flotsam like a crate of strong liquor
                that addles our skis
                & when they bump
                   it's a total fucking gas

KEVIN HART

The Twenty-first Century

When we arrive there
with our guns, our machinery, our heavy books,
there will be so much to say,

and we will sit down
over cigars and cognac and tell our stories
of minor battles, mirages, times when it seemed
no one would survive.

And we will talk only about ourselves,
forgetting our fathers
and all they did, their belief that the future
was only as good
as their plans for it,
and that we grew to be the same.

Then we can finish our stories in peace,
when the wars
are no longer ours to fight,

when we no longer have the clenched fists
of our youth, and our children have inherited
the terrible certainty
that we have ruined all we have been given,

and our hands will be empty,
we will have nothing to give, only our stories
of how everything we should have held before us
like a candle
was lost, forgotten, as we made our way
across the fields of sadness, walking towards the horizon.

Notes on Contributors

ROBERT ADAMSON (1944-) After a confessedly erratic childhood, he worked on a fishing trawler from the Hawkesbury River and spent his adolescence 'Rimbauding up and down the east coast'. A leading figure of the New Romanticism, he has long been closely associated with *New Poetry*. His latest book is *Where I Come From* (1979).

LEX BANNING (1921-65), born in Sydney, was a spastic and triumphed over his disabilities to produce three books of vivid, idiosyncratic verse.

BRUCE BEAVER (1928-) is a poet who has spent almost all of his life in Sydney, with one spell in New Zealand. He assiduously charts the personal townscapes of Manly and environs, and has also written light novels.

JOHN BLIGHT (1913-) is a coastal Queenslander who carried his swag during the Depression. Later an accountant, he has steadily turned into verse the life of the seashore.

CHRISTOPHER BRENNAN (1870-1932) went from a Catholic boyhood to B.A. and M.A. at Sydney University. From two years in Berlin on a travelling scholarship he brought back a German wife and a deep knowledge of French Symbolism. After his major work, *Poems 1913*, his life fell apart despite his versatility of interest and five years as Professor of Comparative Literature at Sydney. Finished on Bohemia's fringes.

R. F. BRISSENDEN (1928-) born Wentworthville, New South Wales, is Reader in English at the Australian National University and has published three books of verse, most recently *Building a Terrace* (1975), and *The Whale in Darkness* (1980).

VINCENT BUCKLEY (1925-   ) was born in Romsey, Victoria, of Irish farming stock and now holds a Personal Chair in English at the University of Melbourne. Long involved in political issues, he has been a challenging literary critic as well as poet. His ideological influence is widely felt.

DAVID CAMPBELL (1915-79) came from a country family, was at Cambridge with John Manifold, played rugby for England and was a distinguished R.A.A.F. pilot in World War II. He lived on a property near Canberra and played a leading part in that city's literary life. A clubbable and well-loved man with a distinctly lucid gift.

GARY CATALANO (1947-   ) was born on the Gold Coast where his Sicilian father worked on a banana plantation. He went to school and later worked in an art gallery in Sydney. He is now a Melburnian, and his study of Australian art in the sixties, *The Years of Hope*, will appear in 1980.

CHRISTINE CHURCHES (1945-   ) grew up in Keith, South Australia, lived in New South Wales and now makes her home in Adelaide. She is married to an Anglican priest and has four children. She writes book reviews, and lectures on poetry for the Department of Continuing Education.

J. M. COUPER (1914-   ) is a Scot who arrived in Australia after the war. He has been a teacher in schools and at Macquarie University, and has written a long narrative poem, *The Book of Bligh* (1969).

BRUCE DAWE (1930-   ) is one of the country's most popular poets, his work reflecting and commenting on many of the attitudes of middle suburbia. Born in Geelong, he has had many jobs, including a long stint in the R.A.A.F. He now teaches English at Toowoomba.

ROSEMARY DOBSON (1920-   ) was born in Sydney and studied art, which has left a strong impression on her poetry. She now lives in Canberra and is involved in the translation of modern Russian poetry.

NOTES ON CONTRIBUTORS

MICHAEL DRANSFIELD (1948-73) His involvement in the narcotic sub-culture along with his early death has made Dransfield into something of a cult figure. His many short lyrics were marked by a precocious brilliance which had little opportunity to develop.

ROBERT D. FITZGERALD (1902-) studied science at Sydney and became a surveyor, at first in Fiji and later back in Australia. He was awarded the O.B.E. in 1951. His most recent book is the entirely characteristic *Product* (1978).

JOHN FORBES was born and lives in Sydney. He edits *Surfers Paradise* and is the author of the unforgettable politico-sporting line, 'the follow-through describes the swing'. An aesthetic ally of John Tranter.

DAME MARY GILMORE, née Cameron (1865-1962), came from rural New South Wales, of Gaelic-speaking stock, and joined William Lane's utopian New Australia colony in Paraguay. For twenty-three years edited woman's page in the Sydney *Worker*. D.B.E., 1936.

MAX HARRIS (1921-), for many years one of the most visible of Australian poets, he has been an avant-gardist, *flâneur*, publisher and columnist. His presence has been felt in the expressionist magazine, *Angry Penguins*, published in Melbourne from 1941 to 1946, and in the inimitable Mary Martin Bookshops.

ROBERT HARRIS (1951-) spent some time in the Western District but now lives in Sydney. He has published three books, most recently *The Abandoned* (1979).

KEVIN HART (1954-) A Londoner by birth, he graduated in Philosophy from the Australian National University, had a Stanford Scholarship to California and now teaches at Geelong College. A leading member of the *Canberra Poetry* group, he has published one collection, *The Departure* (1978).

WILLIAM HART-SMITH (1911-) was born in England, served with the Australian forces in World War II and has since worked at many occupations. One of the early Jindyworobaks, he now lives in Perth.

GWEN HARWOOD (1920-) blossomed late as a poet. Growing up in Brisbane, she has lived since 1945 in Hobart. She has also beguilingly published as Francis Geyer, Walter Lehmann, Miriam Stone and Timothy Kline. She has written a number of opera librettos, most notably *The Fall of the House of Usher* with Larry Sitsky, and she once wrote a scandalous acrostic sonnet.

DOROTHY HEWETT (1923-) recently moved from Perth to Sydney for the second time. Her poetry is radical, sexual and romantic, while she is also a playwright of note. Her latest book of verse is *Greenhouse* (1979).

A. D. HOPE (1907-), the son of a Presbyterian minister, grew up in rural New South Wales and Tasmania, and studied at Sydney and Oxford. He became Professor of English and in 1968 Professor Emeritus at the Australian National University. His first book, *The Wandering Islands*, made a great splash in 1955. Since then he has been widely productive of verse, poetics and criticism. He played a leading part in what J. D. Pringle calls 'the counter-reformation of Australian poetry'. *The New Cratylus* (1979) distils his views on the practice of poetry.

EVAN JONES (1931-) studied History at the University of Melbourne and English under Yvor Winters while on a Creative Writing Fellowship at Stanford. A keen student of the animal kingdom, he teaches English and a course in fairy tales at Melbourne.

GEOFFREY LEHMANN (1940-) is a Sydney lawyer. He has been a close associate of Les Murray since their joint book, *The Ilex Tree* (1965), and was the editor of *Comic Australian Verse* (1972).

JAMES MCAULEY (1917-76) was a poet who gave himself substantially to public life. During the war he worked for the Directorate of Research and Civil Affairs. He was the foundation editor of the right-wing journal, *Quadrant*, and in 1961 was appointed Professor of English in the University of Tasmania. He became a Catholic in 1952, and stood out steadily against modernism in the arts.

HUGH MCCRAE (1876-1958), son of George Gordon McCrae, worked for an architect, but abandoned this to become a writer, illustrator, actor and charmer. Few could resist the personality which comes more strongly through his letters than through his *art nouveau* verse.

RONALD MCCUAIG (1908-) a Sydney journalist, has been one of the wittiest and most inventive of Australian poets.

ROGER MCDONALD (1941-) spent much of his boyhood in New South Wales country towns. After working in schools and for the A.B.C., he was responsible for the University of Queensland Press's very successful poetry programme. He is married to Rhyll McMaster, and has published the highly successful novel *1915* (1979).

KENNETH MACKENZIE (1913-55), a West Australian of precocious talents, was strongly affected by the vitalist influence of Norman Lindsay. He possessed a rich lyrical talent and published four novels of distinction under the name Seaforth Mackenzie. He drowned in a creek near Goulburn.

RHYLL MCMASTER (1947-) comes from Brisbane and was first published as a schoolgirl poet. She was a nurse at the Royal Canberra Hospital and has two daughters. Her one book is *The Brineshrimp* (1972).

DAVID MALOUF (1934-) was brought up in Queensland but has spent long periods in England and Italy, living at present near Grosseto. Lately adding fiction to poetry, he has with his second novel, *An Imaginary Life* (1978), achieved a substantial success.

J. S. MANIFOLD (1915-) has been one of the few Australian poets with Communist sympathies. Educated at Geelong Grammar School and Cambridge, he spent some years in the British Army and now lives in Queensland. An accomplished musician and an authority on folk-music.

LES A. MURRAY (1938-) spent his early years on the family dairy farm near Bunyah, an area he celebrates in his poetry. For some years a translator from various languages, he has called his selected poems *The Vernacular Republic*. He has also sought to use ingredients from the vanishing Aboriginal cultures. His latest book is *The Boys Who Stole the Funeral* (1980).

JOHN SHAW NEILSON (1872-1942) was the very type of the peasant-poet so many critics dream of finding. He had little education and spent most of his life as a poor bush worker. From 1928 he held a minor post at the Country Roads Board in Melbourne. In 1934 his remarkable *Collected Poems* was edited by R. H. Croll.

LEWIS PACKER (1935-), previously Richard Packer, arrived in Australia from New Zealand in 1966 and has worked in advertising. He has written radio plays as well as verse, and seeks a poetry 'that has something approaching objective being'.

VANCE PALMER (1885-1959), short story writer, novelist and an exemplary figure of the secular left. His prose work, *The Legend of the Nineties* (1954) has been profoundly influential.

JAMES PICOT (1906-44) was born in England, studied theology, and died in a Japanese prison camp in Burma. *With a Hawk's Quill* was published by Meanjin Press in 1953.

PETER PORTER (1929-) left Brisbane for London in 1951 and spent ten years in advertising. Now a freelance writer in the English weeklies, his work is permeated by his fascination with European culture, especially opera. He has published seven volumes of poetry.

JENNIFER J. RANKIN (1941-79) was educated at the University of Sydney and wrote plays for stage and radio. Her second book, *Earth Hold* (1979), was jointly produced with the artist, John Olsen.

ELIZABETH RIDDELL (1909-) is an outstanding journalist. She was born in New Zealand and has worked in Australia, the U.S.A. and Europe, where she followed the Allied invasion into France.

ROLAND ROBINSON (1913-) who came out from Ireland as a boy, was also a major figure of the Jindyworobak movement. He has been an instructive collector of Aboriginal folk-lore in prose and verse, a task represented by such books as *The Feathered Serpent* (1956). A bardic presence.

JUDITH RODRIGUEZ née Green (1936-) spent her childhood and adolescence in Brisbane and now teaches in the English Department at La Trobe University. Fascinated by 'composite art forms', she publishes her poetry and her linocuts side by side.

J. R. ROWLAND (1925-) has served as a diplomat in many parts of the globe, and they have left their variegated colours on his verse.

THOMAS W. SHAPCOTT (1935-) has spent most of his life in Ipswich where until recently he practised as an accountant. He is a most prolific poet and a catholic anthologist. He is deeply interested in music, which almost claimed him during his adolescence. In 1978 he won the Canada–Australia Literary Award.

R. A. SIMPSON (1929-), who lives in Murrumbeena, Victoria, has taught art for many years and is at present a Senior Lecturer at the Caulfield Institute of Technology. The shadows of a Catholic boyhood fall across his poetry.

KENNETH SLESSOR (1901-71) was a journalist lifelong and the first Australian poet to learn from the modernist movement. His stature was made fully apparent by *One Hundred Poems 1919-1939*. The poetic silence which shrouded the remainder of his busy life has puzzled all commentators. His prose is collected in *Bread and Wine* (1970).

VIVIAN SMITH (1933-) was born and educated in Hobart, where he lectured in French. He now teaches English at the University of Sydney and is Literary Editor of *Quadrant*.

PETER STEELE, S.J. (1938-), comes from Perth, was for some years Rector of Campion College, lectures at Melbourne University and has published a study of Swift. Noted for his generous wit.

DOUGLAS STEWART (1913-), who came to Sydney from New Zealand in 1938, has been one of the most influential figures in modern Australian writing, chiefly in his role as literary editor of the *Bulletin* but also at the publishing house of Angus and Robertson. He has made his name not only as a lyric poet but also as a verse dramatist, with such works as *Ned Kelly* (1943).

HAROLD STEWART (1916-) was for many years closely associated with James McAuley with whom he invented the surrealist poetic prodigy, Ern Malley. A student of oriental culture, he now lives in Kyoto, Japan.

RANDOLPH STOW (1935-) was brought up in Western Australia but has restlessly moved from place to place, from occupation to occupation. He now lives in rural Suffolk. His talent showed itself early in poetry, five distinctive novels and a hilarious children's book, *Midnite* (1967).

ANDREW TAYLOR (1940-) grew up in seaside Warrnambool and later spent a couple of years in Italy. He lectures at the University of Adelaide and has published five volumes of poetry.

NOTES ON CONTRIBUTORS

JOHN TRANTER (1943-) was born at Cooma, like A. D. Hope. He has been involved in editing and radio production. His disconcerting books of verse include *The Alphabet Murders* (1975) and *Crying in Early Infancy: One Hundred Sonnets* (1978).

CLIVE TURNBULL (1906-75) was born and educated in Tasmania, worked as a journalist and published variously on art and Australian history.

KATH WALKER (1920-) is the first Aboriginal poet to become widely known in English. A member of the Noonuccal tribe, she is prominent in the political stirrings of her people.

CHRIS WALLACE-CRABBE (1934-), who grew up in Melbourne, has lived in Europe and America at different times. He has published a dozen books of poetry and criticism.

ALAN WEARNE (1948-) is a lifelong devotee of suburban manners. He was a Labor candidate for the Legislative Council at the last Victorian State election. He has published two books and his dramatic monologues are marked by the most original style in Australian poetry.

FRANCIS WEBB (1925-73), born in Adelaide, lived in Sydney, Canada, England and New South Wales again. He spent many years in hospital, a fact to which his dense, brilliant, anguished poetry bears witness. His Catholic faith is strongly present in his writing. Hailed as a forebear by many of the younger poets.

SUSAN WHITING (1947-) graduated B.Arch. from Melbourne University in 1970 and practised for a few years in Melbourne and London. She lives on a farm at Rocky Hall, New South Wales, with poet Allen Afterman and their son, Adam.

JUDITH WRIGHT (1915-) is a poet from pioneering rural stock. Brought up near Armidale, she has explored her family background in a prose study, *The Generations of Men* (1959). An extremely versatile poet, she has recently become a forthright spokesman for the conservationist movement in Queensland and New South Wales, and now lives on a wild-life sanctuary near Braidwood.

FAY ZWICKY (1933-) was a musical prodigy during her Melbourne childhood and later a concert pianist. At present she is Senior Lecturer in English at the University of Western Australia.

Acknowledgements

The editor and publishers wish to thank the following, who have given their permission to reproduce copyright poems:

Angus & Robertson Publishers Ltd: Mary Gilmore, 'Nationality' and 'An Aboriginal Simile' from *Selected Verse*; Christopher Brennan, 'The Wanderer' and 'The point of noon is past' from *The Verse of Christopher Brennan*; John Shaw Neilson, 'The Orange Tree', 'May', 'Native Companions Dancing' and 'Song Be Delicate' from *The Poems of Shaw Neilson*; Hugh McCrae, 'Fragment' from *The Best Poems of Hugh McCrae*; Kenneth Slessor, 'The Night-Ride', 'South Country', 'Captain Dobbin', 'Sleep', 'Five Bells' and 'Beach Burial' from *Poems*; R. D. FitzGerald, 'The Face of the Waters', 'Fifth Day' and 'Beginnings' from *Forty Years' Poems*, and 'Height' from *Product*; A. D. Hope, 'Australia', 'Ascent into Hell', 'Imperial Adam' and 'The Double Looking Glass' from *Collected Poems, 1930-1970*, and 'In Memoriam: Gertrud Kolmar, 1943' from *A Late Picking*; Ronald McCuaig, 'The Commercial Traveller's Wife' from *Quod Ronald McCuaig*, and '*Au Tombeau de mon père*' from *The Ballad of Bloodthirsty Bessie and Other Poems*; W. Hart-Smith, 'Black Stockman', 'Space' and 'Traffic' from *Poems of Discovery*; Roland Robinson, 'I had no Human Speech' and 'The Myth and the Mountain' from *Deep Well*; Kenneth Mackenzie, 'The Moonlit Doorway', 'Two Trinities' and 'An Old Inmate' from *Poems*; Douglas Stewart, 'Terra Australis', 'The Snow-Gum', 'The Silkworms' and 'B Flat' from *Collected Poems, 1936-1967*; David Campbell, 'Men in Green', 'Windy Gap', 'Dear Maurice', 'Mothers and Daughters' and 'The Australian Dream' from *Selected Poems*; Judith Wright, 'Brother and Sisters', 'South of My Days', 'Woman to Man', 'Train Journey' and 'Extinct Birds' from *Collected Poems, 1942-1970*, and 'Some Words' from *Alive: Poems, 1970-1972*; Harold Stewart, 'A Flight of Wild Geese' from *Phoenix Wings*; James McAuley, 'Envoi for a Book of Poems', 'The Incarnation of Sirius', 'Invocation' and

237

ACKNOWLEDGEMENTS

'Because' from *Collected Poems, 1936-1970*; Rosemary Dobson, 'The Bystander' and 'Country Press' from *Selected Poems*; Gwen Harwood, 'I am the Captain of My Soul', 'In Brisbane', 'All Souls' and 'Person to Person' from *Selected Poems*; Vincent Buckley, extracts from *Golden Builders*; J. R. Rowland, 'In Southeast Asia' from *The Feast of Ancestors*; Francis Webb, 'For My Grandfather', 'Dawn Wind on the Islands', 'Morgan's Country', 'A Death at Winson Green' and 'Harry' from *Collected Poems*; Vivian Smith, 'At an Exhibition of Historical Paintings, Hobart' from *An Island South*; Chris Wallace-Crabbe, 'A Wintry Manifesto' and 'An Allegiance' from *Selected Poems*, and 'Introspection' and 'Old Men during a Fall of Government' from *The Emotions are not Skilled Workers*; Randolph Stow, 'Dust' and 'Ruins of the City of Hay' from *A Counterfeit Silence: Selected Poems*; Les A. Murray, 'A New England Farm, August 1914', 'An Absolutely Ordinary Rainbow', 'Senryu', 'The Ballad of Jimmy Governor' and 'The Buladelah-Taree Holiday Song Cycle' from *Selected Poems: the Vernacular Republic*; Geoffrey Lehmann, 'Out after Dark' and 'The Telescope at Siding Springs' from *Selected Poems*; Andrew Taylor, 'Cosimo' from *The Cat's Chin and Ears: a Bestiary*; John Tranter, extract from *The Alphabet Murders*; Christine Churches, 'Autumn — for My Son' from *My Mother and the Trees*; and John Forbes, 'Ode to Tropical Skiing' from *Tropical Skiing*. Australian National University Press for 'Language, Talk to Me', by Evan Jones. Mrs Anne Banning for the poems by Lex Banning. Big Smoke Books for the poems by Robert Adamson and Dorothy Hewett. Mr John Blight and the *Age* for 'The Bone'. Dr R. F. Brissenden for 'The Death of Damiens'. Mr C. B. Christesen for James Picot's 'For It Was Early Summer'. Dr J. M. Couper for his version of 'Horace, Odes, I, 5'. Mr Max Harris for his two poems. Mr Robert Harris for 'Tobacco'. Mr Kevin Hart and *Poetry Australia* for 'The Twenty-first Century'. The Hawthorn Press for 'Living/Dying' by Peter Steele. Jacaranda Press for 'We are going' by Kath Walker. Longman Cheshire Pty Ltd for the poems by Bruce Dawe. Oxford University Press, London, for 'An Exequy', 'Non piangere, Liù' and 'In the New World happiness is allowed', by Peter Porter. To Mr Peter Porter for his 'Sydney Cove, 1788' and 'The Last of England'. Mr David Rankin for 'Green Ash' by Jennifer J. Rankin. Miss Elizabeth Riddell for 'Country Tune'. Mr R. A. Simpson for his three poems. South Head Press for the two poems by Bruce Beaver. Mr R. Grant Taylor and the estate of the late Vance Palmer for 'The Farmer remembers the Somme'. Mrs J. Turnbull for 'Lost Love' by Clive Turnbull. University of Queensland Press: for the poems from *Collected Verse* by J. S. Manifold, published by University of Queensland Press, 1978; for the poems from *Bicycle*, 1970, and *Neighbours in a Thicket*, 1974, by David Malouf published by University of Queensland Press; for the poem from *Being out of Order* by Richard Packer, published by University

ACKNOWLEDGEMENTS

of Queensland Press, 1972; for the poems from *Begin with Walking*, 1972, and *Selected Poems*, 1978, by Thomas W. Shapcott published by University of Queensland Press; for the two poems from *Water Life* by Judith Rodriguez, published by University of Queensland Press in 1976; for the poem from *Airship* by Roger McDonald published by University of Queensland Press in 1975; for the poem from *Remembering the Rural Life* by Gary Catalano published by University of Queensland Press in 1978; for the poems by Rhyll McMaster from *the brineshrimp* published by University of Queensland Press in 1972; for the poem from *Streets of the Long Voyage* by Michael Dransfield published by University of Queensland Press in 1970 (reprinted 1972 and 1974); and for 'The Nocturne in the Corner Phonebox' from *The Cool Change* by Andrew Taylor published by University of Queensland Press in 1971. Mr Alan Wearne for his two poems. Ms Susan Whiting and the *Age* for 'Sifting Stones at Capri'. Ms Fay Zwicky for 'Summer Pogrom'.

Index of First Lines